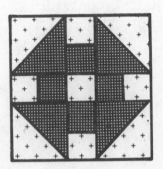
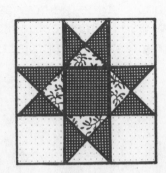

From the Quilt in a Day™ Series

T·R·I·O

of Treasured Quilts

by Eleanor Burns

To Great Aunt Edna — and your Glorious Feed Sacks!

You have long been gone, but the memory of you and your feed sacks still live on. How well I remember picking out just the perfect tiny prints for my first sewing projects.

FRONT COVER
Bear's Paw quilt by Patricia Knoechel
Monkey Wrench pillow and Ohio Star quilt by Eleanor Burns

Illustrations by Patricia Knoechel
Photography by Jon Hansen and Wayne Norton
Printing by A & L Litho, Escondido, CA

First Edition - October, 1983
Copyright © 1983 by Eleanor Burns
Second Edition - January, 1990
Copyright © 1990 by Eleanor Burns

ISBN 0-922705-09-7

Contents

INTRODUCTION

The older I get, the more appreciative I become of "old things." In the summer of 1983, I visited my family in Pennsylvania and had the chance to ramble around the countryside exploring vintage clothing stores and antique shops.

Oh what pleasure that log cabin and old barn I discovered stuffed full of antiques brought me! I remember the excitement I felt to touch this perfect blue and cream Monkey Wrench quilt made by some fine Amish woman with its dark blue "humility block" in the corner. Yet the price on it was something I couldn't afford. . .and that's why I make my own quilts!

I love quilts; I love to choose the colors and touch the cotton fabrics. I feel tranquil when I sew quilts. I feel a rush of love as I tuck the cotton around my boys at night. The quilt on my own bed has seen me through the lights and darks of life. Quilts fill up lonely spots on the walls in my home.

You should have the same pleasures over making and giving your quilts as I do. I'm pleased to present these simple, fast sewing techniques in quiltmaking to you. With the Trio of Treasured Quilts, they will go together so quickly and easily, that you will be able to make and give a variety of quilts to all your favorite ones. Enjoy!

Chapter 1

How to Use
the Trio of Treasured Quilts

There are three different patterns in *the Trio of Treasured Quilts:*

Monkey Wrench   Ohio Star   Bear's Paw

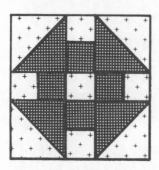 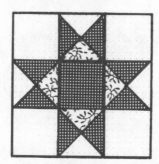 

The quilts were meant to have only one pattern per quilt repeated throughout for a total look. The three different patterns were not meant to be mixed together as in a Sampler quilt. Although I do not give instructions, the tops are perfect for hand quilting.

1. Familiarize yourself with the Table of Contents. Use it to locate specific pages.

2. Read through the general sewing terms and supplies. All cutting and sewing techniques in *the Trio* are based on this information, and therefore are absolutely essential to read. (Chapters 2 and 3)

3. Decide on the specific project you want to make, or the size quilt you need. You may feel more comfortable sewing a country decorating project or lap robe rather than a king size quilt for your first project.

4. Decide which pattern you want to make. The Skill Level Guide on page 12 will guide you. Select the Monkey Wrench or Ohio Star if you are new to sewing patchwork.

5. *The Trio of Treasured Quilts* is coded beside the page numbers with the pattern pictures pertinent to that section. As you thumb through the book, you can quickly identify the section with the information you need. All patterns will be pictured when the information is appropriate for all three.

6. Country Decorating Projects. Most of these use just one block. Their yardages are found on:

Monkey Wrench	Page 31
Ohio Star	Page 53
Bear's Paw	Page 75

Purchase the additional materials and supplies needed to complete the project. (Chapter 15)

7. Quilts: Decide if you want your quilt to have lattice and cornerstones or patchwork and solid blocks. Purchase the yardage for your specific pattern, plus all additional purchases. (Chapter 4)

8. Cut your purchased yardage into specific sizes for each pattern and quilt size. Follow the Cutting Charts provided. Monkey Wrench (Chapter 5), Ohio Star (Chapter 6), Bear's Paw (Chapter 7)

9. Sew all the pieces with multiple assembly techniques. Follow the specific instructions for each pattern. Monkey Wrench (Chapter 5), Ohio Star (Chapter 6), Bear's Paw (Chapter 7)

10. Sew all the pieces into blocks with multiple assembly techniques. (Chapter 9)

11. Set the quilt top together with Lattice and Cornerstones (Chapter 10) or set it together with Patchwork and Solid Blocks. (Chapter 11)

12. Sew on the borders. (Chapter 12)

13. Finish your quilt. (Chapter 13)

Chapter 2

General Sewing Terms

Color Selection

The Monkey Wrench uses only light and dark calicos. The Ohio Star and Bear's Paw combines lights, mediums and darks.

For very dramatic looking patterns, I like to use colors that are very different in their color tones.

Each section gives specific suggestions for colors appropriate for that block.

Once you choose just the colors of your light, medium and dark, this is another good rule to follow. Combine one large scale print and two small scale prints, or one large scale print, one small scale print, and one solid. A micro dot can be used as a solid fabric to give a more "peaceful" feeling to the block. Use a border print stripe with rather "quiet" blocks to brighten the quilt.

Cutting

Use a rotary cutter, gridded cutting board, and a variety of plexiglas rulers (6'' x 24'', 12½'' x 12½'', and 6'' x 6''). Fabrics that are cut into the same size pieces and sewn right sides together can be layered and cut right sides together.

Cut long, narrow strips and large rectangles with the rotary cutter and 6'' x 24'' ruler on a gridded board. Ill. 1

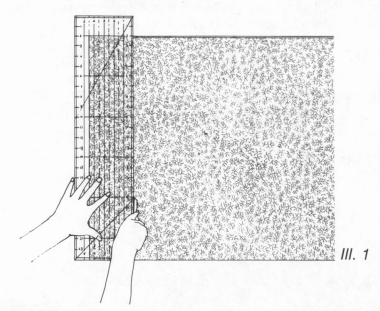

Ill. 1

Use the 12½" square ruler for cutting rectangles and squares less than 12½". Ill. 2

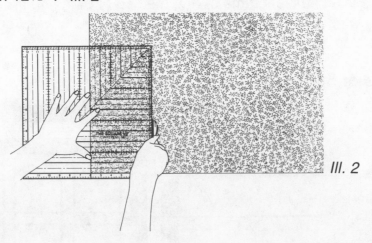

Ill. 2

Squares less than 6" can easily be cut from long narrow strips first cut with the 6" x 24" ruler, and then cut with the 6" square ruler. Stack several strips on top of each other. Cut the squares from the selvage edge toward the center fold. Ill. 3

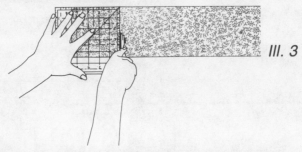

Ill. 3

On each quilt, cut the first measurement the width of the fabric from selvage to selvage. Cut that piece into the second measurement.

Finger Pin

Match the ends of blocks by squeezing them together between your fingers. Do not use actual pins.

Flashfeed

Pick up the first two pairs of blocks and place them right sides together. Sew the first pair together. Do not raise the presser foot or clip the threads. Butt and stitch the second pair immediately behind the first. Butt and stitch all pairs together in the same manner.

Horizontal Rows

This is sewing rows of blocks together in a left to right direction. See a complete description in Chapter 9: Multiple Assembly Sewing of the Pieces into Blocks.

Multiple Assembly

This is an efficient, time saving method of planning for, cutting and sewing many blocks at once. All blocks are worked on and completed at the same time.

Parts of the Quilt

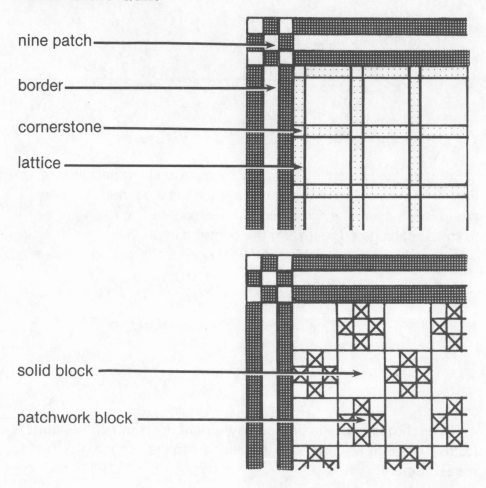

nine patch

border

cornerstone

lattice

solid block

patchwork block

Pressing

Do not open up the pieces. Place on the ironing board with the light sides on the bottom. Drop one piece in the center of the ironing board. Lift up the dark part and press it open and flat. Do not put down the iron. Lay a second piece on top of the first with light side down again. Press open and flat. Continue to press without putting down the iron. Stack in order as you press the pieces.

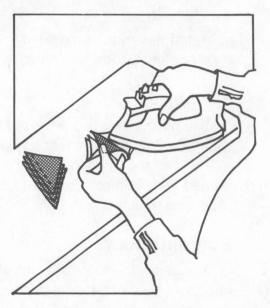

Seam Allowance

Use a ¼'' seam allowance throughout all sewing. The seam allowance is already added to all patterns and does not need to be added. Using a general purpose presser foot similar to this is excellent as a guide. Adjust your sewing machine needle so that the measurement from the needle to the edge of the presser foot is ¼''. Test your ¼'' seam by sewing on a piece of ¼'' graph paper without thread in the machine.

Skill Level

This is a guide based on ability to help you choose which quilt you wish to make.

Elementary — Monkey Wrench
Intermediate — Ohio Star
Advanced — Bear's Paw

If you are an inexperienced sewer or wish to make a quilt quickly, select the Monkey Wrench or Ohio Star. However, even the advanced pattern, Bear's Paw, is fairly easy and fun to sew — it just takes longer.

Stitches Per Inch

Use 15 stitches per inch. Since this is a tight stitch, the thread ends will not pull out if they have not been back stitched. Also, the end threads are generally stitched over in the next step to further lock them.

Stitch in the Ditch *(Place bonded batting behind the patchwork.)*

This is a machine method of adding quilting depth and dimension to the pattern. Place the block underneath the presser foot, lower the needle at the • marked on the patterns symbolizing the starting point. Following the direction of the arrow, machine sew through all thicknesses in the "ditch" of the seam.

The machine stitching brings out the graphic design in each pattern.

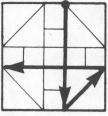 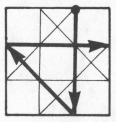 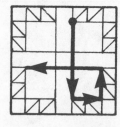

Monkey Wrench   Ohio Star   Bear's Paw

Tearing to Put Your Fabric on the Straight of Grain

This method works well on 100% cotton fabrics. Straighten the fabric by taking a nick 1" in on the selvage edge and tearing it across the fabric to the other selvage. Keep on nicking and tearing until you have one complete strip from selvage to selvage. Tear off the tightly woven selvage edge.

Vertical Rows

This is sewing the pieces together into one block in a top to bottom, left to right direction. See Chapter 9, Multiple Assembly Sewing of the Pieces into Blocks, for complete thorough instructions with illustrations.

13

Chapter 3

Fabrics, Notions and Supplies

Calico Prints

The yardage charts are based on 45" width small calico prints. Select a good grade of closely woven 100% cottons. A good quality fabric makes a lasting quilt.

Preshrink your calicos by rinsing and drying them.

Backing

Yardage and measurements are given for using 45" width fabrics. Lengths will need to be pieced to the same size as the quilt top.

Bonded Batting

The batting must be 100% bonded polyester so that it does not fall apart inside your quilt.

It is generally sold two different ways:

1) Prepackaged: The batting is one big sheet when it is unfolded, and generally of a thin (½") to medium (¾") thickness. Package instructions say to let it fill with air one day before using it. Buy a size larger than the size quilt you wish to make.

2) By the Yard: This batting is generally 48" wide and a medium (¾") to thick (1") depth. The yardage charts are based on a 48" width. However, some limited stores now have available a very thick (1") batting 54" in width. The thicker batting produces a more dimensional looking, warm quilt.

Choose a thin batting if you are going to finish with machine quilting. Choose a very thick or even double batting for a comforter look, and tie all the thicknesses together.

Feel the batting and wrap in it when you are purchasing it. It should bend with you, rather than stand stiff.

Batting can be pieced by butting two pieces up beside each other and hand whip-stitching or machine zig-zag stitching them together. The batting trimmings can be used for stuffing pillows and toys.

Gridded Cutting Board

Use a special plastic gridded cutting board when marking grid lines on large fabric pieces and when cutting with the rotary cutter.

Rotary Cutter

This is an industrial size, hand cutting tool capable of cutting through several layers of fabric at one time. It rolls over the fabric and cuts much like a pizza cutter. The rotary cutter should be used with a plexiglas ruler on a special plastic gridded mat.

Rulers

Use a 6'' x 24'' plexiglas ruler for marking and cutting grid lines on large pieces of fabric, a 6'' square ruler for cutting and squaring up pieces smaller than 6'', and a 12½'' square ruler for cutting and squaring up pieces and blocks larger than 6''.

Thread

Sew the quilt blocks together with a good quality of neutral shade polyester spun thread.

Needles

Use a number 14 or 80 needle made especially for woven fabrics. Do not use a ball point needle. A curved needle generally used for carpets and upholstery is excellent for tying quilts together.

Pins

Use extra long straight pins with large heads when pinning the layers of fabric and batting together.

Yarn

Use wool yarn or ¹⁄₁₆'' ribbon for tying the face of the quilt to the backing if you are interested in a bolder look. All six strands of embroidery floss, crochet thread or pearl cotton have a softer look.

Marker

Use a sharp pencil that produces fine lines. Make certain that you do not use a dark one that will show up behind the light calicos once the blocks are sewn.

Presser Foot

Use a multipurpose foot in which the needle hits the center of the opening, which has equal sides for accurate ¼'' sewing.

Chapter 4

Yardage Charts

Yardage for the Quilts

The yardage and illustrations are given for crib, lap, twin, double, queen, and king size quilts. You can make any of the three patterns into quilts with lattice and cornerstones or quilts with patchwork and solid blocks. Sizes do vary between the two styles. The quilts with the solid blocks and patchwork are definitely easier to make with less sewing time and less corners to match.

The quilts are coverlet size: the blocks cover the top of the mattress and the borders hang over the sides, covering the first mattress. If you want your quilt to hang to the floor, buy the yardage for the next size quilt. As you are sewing your blocks, lay them on the mattress and see if you are getting the fit you want. Add more rows of blocks to get the desired size.

Yardage for One Block

I highly recommend making just one block before purchasing the yardage for your whole quilt to test your colors and to try the sewing methods. The yardages for just one block are on:

> Monkey Wrench — 31
>
> Ohio Star — 53
>
> Bear's Paw — 75

The three different patterns were not meant to be mixed together as in a Sampler Quilt.

All three patterns are not the same finished size. The Monkey Wrench and the Ohio Star are very near the same size. However, the Bear's Paw is definitely larger! It was my original plan that all three would be the same size, but as I worked with the original Bear's Paw pieces, they were so tiny I didn't enjoy sewing with them. I couldn't honestly tell you that you would enjoy sewing with them!

Crib Quilt

 *Shaded Area Represents Patchwork*

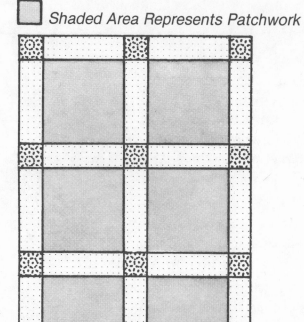

Lattice and Cornerstones

Approximate Finished Size:
33" x 48"

Six Blocks
2 x 3

Patchwork and Solid Blocks

Approximate Finished Size:
42" x 42"

Nine Blocks
3 x 3

Five Patchwork Blocks
Four Solid Blocks

Select your pattern and purchase the yardage as listed.

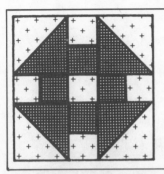
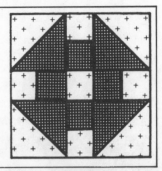

1 yd. light calico
1 yd. dark calico

See Page 29 for color variations.

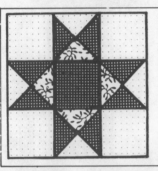
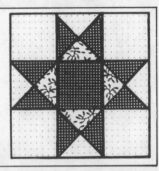

1 yd. light calico
½ yd. medium calico
¾ yd. dark calico

See Page 51 for color variations.

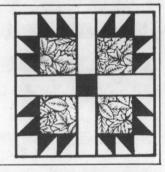

1¼ yd. light calico
⅝ yd. medium calico
¾ yd. dark calico

See Page 73 for color variations.

Additional Purchases for any Pattern

	Quilts with Lattice/ Cornerstones	Quilts with Patchwork and Solid Blocks
Lattice Strips	¾ yd. medium	—
Cornerstones	¼ yd. dark	—
Solid Blocks	—	⅞ yd. medium
Borders	—	⅔ yd. dark
Backing	1½ yds.	1½ yds.
Bonded Batting . . .	1 yd.	1¼ yds.
Pregathered Wide Lace (optional)	4¾ yds.	5 yds.
Yarn, Embroidery Floss, or Pearl Cotton	2 skeins	2 skeins

Lap Robe

Shaded Area Represents Patchwork

Lattice and Cornerstones

Approximate Finished Size:
57" x 72"

Six Blocks
2 x 3

Patchwork and Solid Blocks

Approximate Finshed Size:
60" x 72"

Twelve Blocks
Six Patchwork Blocks
Six Solid Blocks

Select your pattern and purchase the yardage as listed.

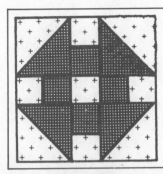 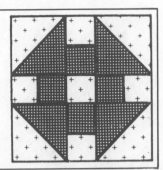

1 yd. light calico
1 yd. dark calico

See Page 29 for color variations.

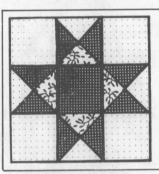 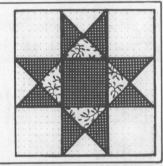

1 yd. light calico.
½ yd. medium calico
¾ yd. dark calico

See Page 51 for color variations.

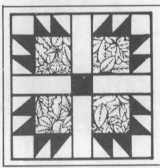 

1¼ yd. light calico
⅝ yd. medium calico
¾ yd. dark calico

See Page 73 for color variations.

Additional Purchases for any Pattern

	Quilts with Lattice/Cornerstones	Quilts with Patchwork and Solid Blocks
Lattice Strips	¾ yd. medium	—
Cornerstones	¼ yd. dark	—
Solid Blocks	—	⅞ yd. medium
Borders	¾ yd. light	¾ yd. light
	½ yd. medium	⅓ yd. medium
	1¾ yds. dark	1¾ yds. dark
Backing	3½ yds.	3½ yds.
Bonded Batting . . .	3½ yd.	3½ yds.
Pregathered Wide Lace (optional)	7½ yds.	8 yds.
Yarn, Embroidery Floss, or Pearl Cotton	2 skeins	2 skeins

20

Twin Quilt

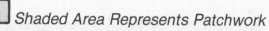
Shaded Area Represents Patchwork

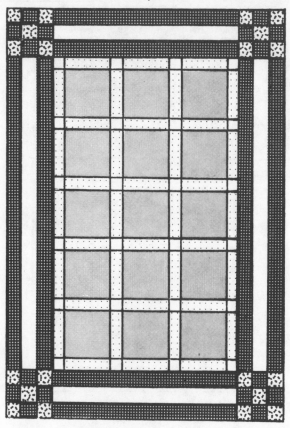

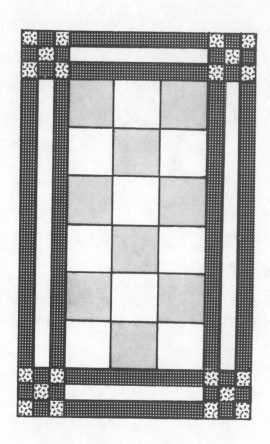

Lattice and Cornerstones

Approximate Finished Size:
72" x 102"

Fifteen Blocks
3 x 5

Patchwork and Solid Blocks

Approximate Finished Size:
60" x 96"

Eighteen Blocks
3 x 6

Nine Patchwork Blocks
Nine Solid Blocks

Select your pattern and purchase the yardage as listed.

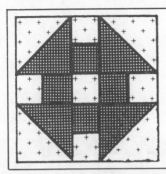 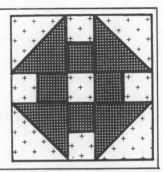

1⅔ yds. light calico
1½ yds. dark calico

See Page 29 for color variations.

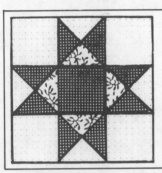 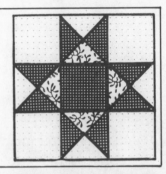

1¾ yds. light calico
⅝ yd. medium calico
1⅜ yds. dark calico

See Page 51 for color variations.

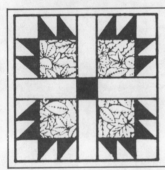 

2¼ yds. light calico
1⅛ yds. medium calico
1¼ yds. dark calico

See Page 73 for color variations.

Additional Purchases for any Pattern

	Quilts with Lattice/ Cornerstones	Quilts with Patchwork and Solid Blocks
Lattice Strips	1½ yd. medium	—
Cornerstones	⅓ yd. dark	—
Solid Blocks	—	1¼ yds. medium
Borders	1¼ yds. light	⅞ yd. light
	½ yd. medium	⅓ yd. medium
	2⅓ yds. dark	2 yds. dark
Backing	6 yds.	5¾ yds.
Bonded Batting . . .	6 yds.	5¾ yds.
Pregathered Wide Lace (optional)	10 yds.	9 yds.
Yarn, Embroidery Floss, or Pearl Cotton	3 skeins	3 skeins

Double — Queen Quilts

Both the double and queen have the same number of blocks in them. However, the borders are 6" wider in the queen than in the double.

Shaded Area Represents Patchwork

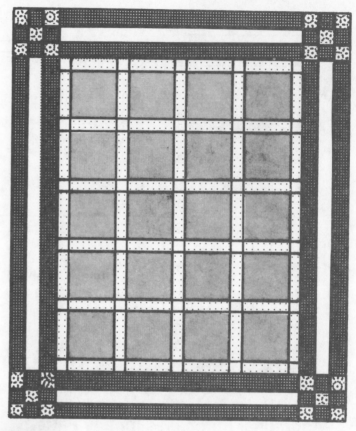

Lattice and Cornerstones...

Approximate Finished Size:
Double — 87" x 102"
Queen — 93" x 108"

Twenty Blocks
4 x 5

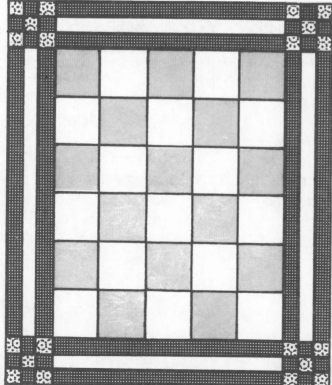

...Patchwork and Solid Blocks

Approximate Finished Size
Double — 84" x 96"
Queen — 90" x 102"

Thirty Blocks
5 x 6

Fifteen Patchwork Blocks
Fifteen Solid Blocks

Select your pattern and purchase the yardage as listed.

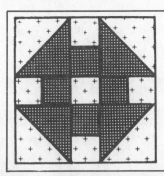 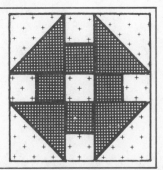

2 yds. light calico
1⅞ yds. dark calico

See Page 29 for color variations.

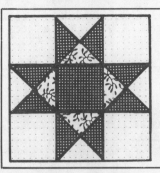 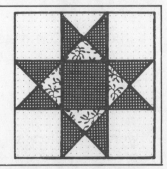

2½ yds. light calico
¾ yd. medium calico
1⅞ yds. dark calico

See Page 51 for color variations.

2½ yds. light calico
1¼ yds. medium calico
1½ yds. dark calico

See Page 73 for color variations.

Additional Purchases for any Pattern

	Quilts with Lattice/ Cornerstones	Quilts with Patchwork and Solid Blocks
Lattice Strips	1¾ yd. medium	—
Cornerstones	½ yd. dark	—
Solid Blocks	—	2 yds. medium
Borders	1¼ yds. (1½) light	1¼ yds. (1½) light
Yardage for	½ yd. (⅝) medium	⅓ yd. (⅝) medium
Queen in ( )	2½ yds. (3) dark	2½ yds. (3) dark
Backing..........	6½ yds. (9½)	5¾ yds. (6)
Bonded Batting ...	6 yds. (6½)	5¾ yds. (6)
Pregathered Wide Lace (optional)	11 yds. (11½)	10½ yds. (11)
Yarn, Embroidery Floss, or Pearl Cotton	5 skeins	5 skeins

24

King Quilt

Lattice and Cornerstones...

Approximate Finished Size:
102" x 102"

Twenty-five Blocks
5 x 5

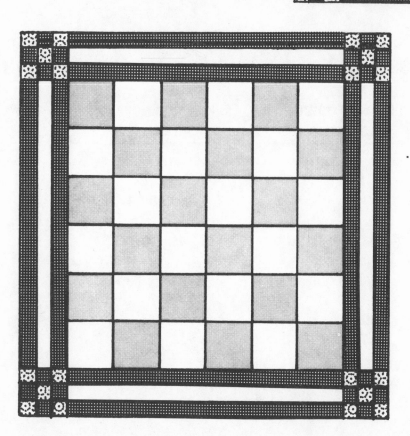

...Patchwork and Solid Blocks

Approximate Finished Size:
96" x 96"

Thirty-six Blocks
6 x 6

Eighteen Patchwork Blocks
Eighteen Solid Blocks

Select your pattern and purchase the yardage as listed.

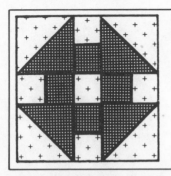
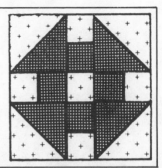

2¾ yds. light calico
2½ yds. dark calico

See Page 29 for color variations.

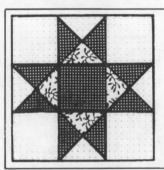
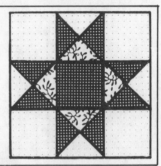

2½ yds. light calico
1 yd. medium calico
2⅛ yds. dark calico

See Page 51 for color variations.

3¼ yds. light calico
1¾ yds. medium calico
1⅞ yds. dark calico

See Page 73 for color variations.

Additional Purchases for any Pattern

	Quilts with Lattice/ Cornerstones	Quilts with Patchwork and Solid Blocks
Lattice Strips	2¼ yds. medium	—
Cornerstones	⅜ yd. dark	—
Solid Blocks	—	2½ yds. medium
Borders	1⅓ yds. light	1⅓ yds. light
	½ yd. medium	⅓ yd. medium
	2¾ yds. dark	2¾ yds. dark
Backing	8½ yds.	8½ yds.
Bonded Batting	6 yds.	6 yds.
Pregathered Wide Lace (optional)	11 yds.	11 yds.
Yarn, Embroidery Floss, or Pearl Cotton	6 skeins	6 skeins

Monkey Wrench

Chapter 5

History

The Monkey Wrench pattern, also known as Churn Dash, Lover's Knot, or Hole in the Barn Door, copies an adjustable-jaw tool important in early households and still used today.

Color Selection

The yardage charts and sewing directions are written for using the same lights and darks throughout the quilt with newly purchased fabric. However, with the simplicity in design, there are many variations in color you may choose to add excitement to your Monkey Wrench quilt.

Some of the most gorgeous Monkey Wrench quilts I have seen were old ones made from scraps that combined dark checks and stripes with light figures similar to fabrics in men's cotton underwear and dress shirts.

When purchasing fabric, perhaps some of these suggested combinations will appeal to you.

light	dark	border	cornerstone
rose calico	blue calico	solid burgundy	striped
gray calico	burgundy calico	solid navy	microdot
camel calico	dark green calico	solid rust	large flower

For combining prints effectively, you may wish to use one large scaled print, one small scaled print, and a solid color. The yardage for just one block is given so you can test your color choices before purchasing fabric for a whole quilt.

Color Variations

When purchasing fabric for a quilt, you may choose several different lights and darks to add color and variety to your finished project. Divide your yardage by the number of variations you wish to have. Set the finished blocks together in alternating order.

Use two different lights. Divide the light yardage in thirds. Use ⅓ for the small squares and ⅔'s for the large triangles.

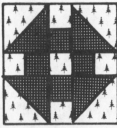

Use a striped fabric for one dark fabric. Use the same striped fabric in the cornerstone.

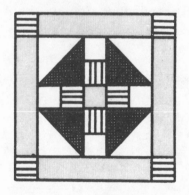

3⅛" x 12½" strips

Use two different darks. Divide the dark yardage in thirds. Use ⅓ for the small squares and ⅔'s for the large triangles.

Use a striped print for one color. See the color Ill. on the apron, inside front cover.

 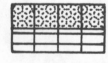

Line up your 6" square ruler diagonally along a line.

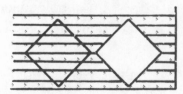

Enhance a plain block with a striped pattern for the lattice.

Change the light in the center. Purchase an additional ¼ yd. light or medium for this change. Consider using this same fabric in the border or cornerstone.

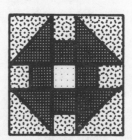

Reverse the light with the dark and make the same number of each in the quilt. Arrange them in alternating order.

Use a solid colored fabric with a calico print.

Use a large scale print with a small scale print or solid fabric.

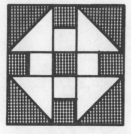

Materials for One Monkey Wrench Block

Skill Level: Elementary
Approximate Finished Size: 12¼" Square
Approximate Construction Time: 30 minutes

Buy:

    ⅓ yd. light calico

    ⅓ yd. dark calico

Cut . . . . **To Make:**

☐ one — 3⅛" x 13" light
☐ one — 3⅛" x 13" dark 4

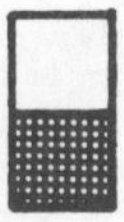

☐ one — 3⅛" square light 1

☐ one — 6" x 12" light
☐ one — 6" x 12" dark 4

Once the pieces are cut, you can check them off in the space provided on the chart.

Sample Paste-Up Block — Paste in your fabric swatches.

light calico

dark calico

variation (optional)

cornerstone

and

lattice

or

solid block

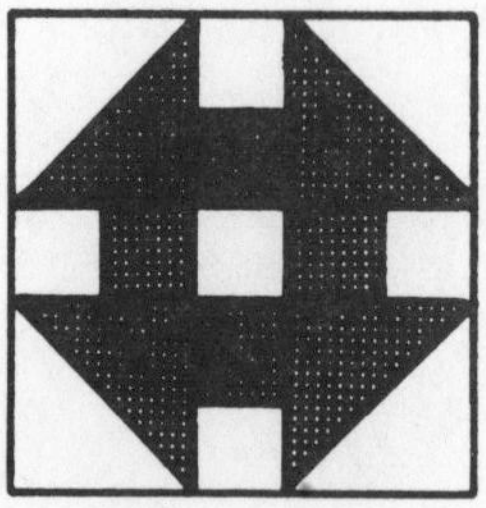

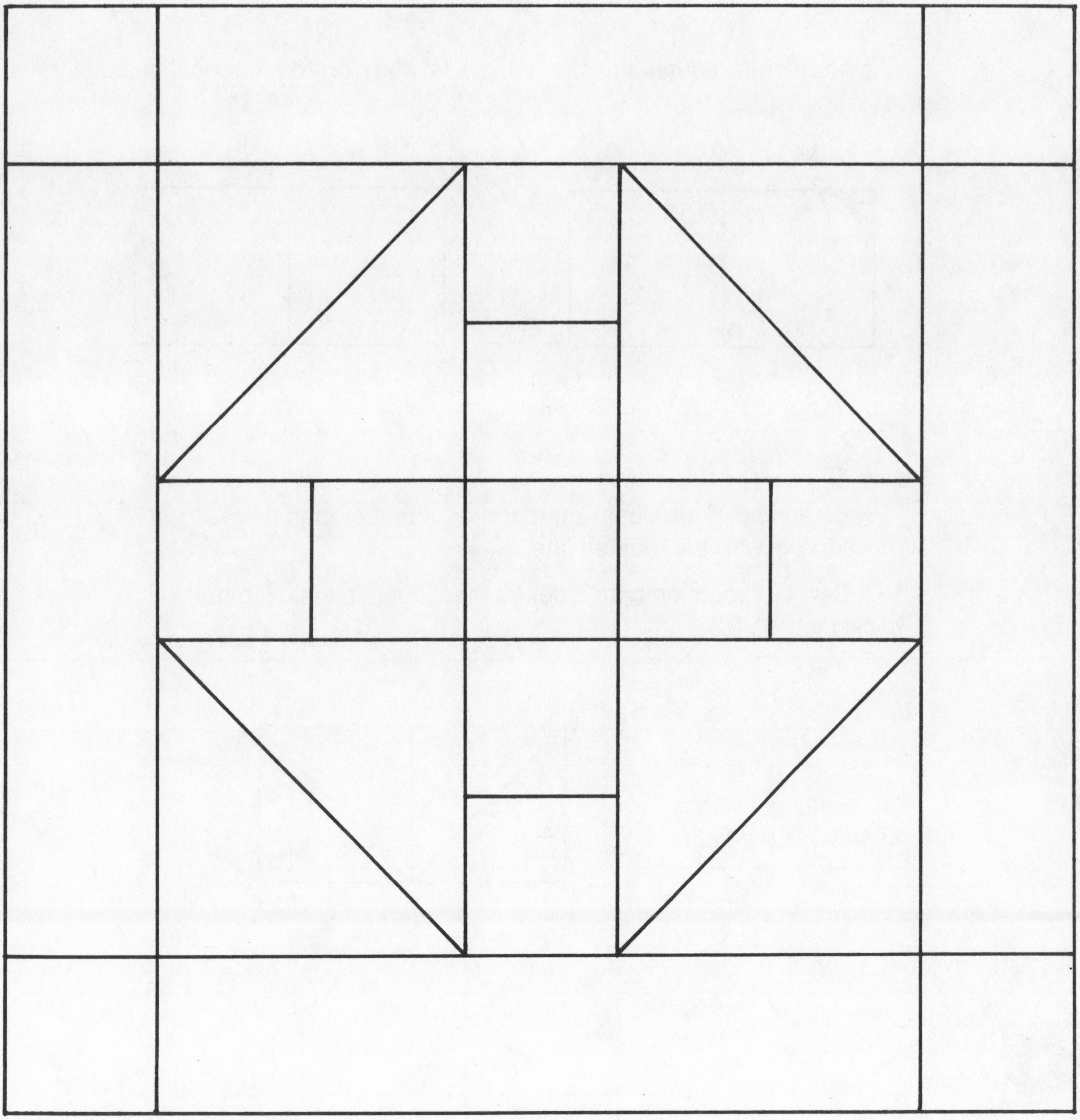

Sewing the Pieces for
One Monkey Wrench Block

Making the  :

1. Place the 6" x 12" light calico and the 6" x 12" dark calico right sides together.

2. Press.

3. Mark on 6" square lines.
Ill. 1

4. Mark on the diagonal lines.
Ill. 2

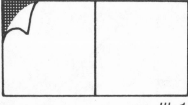

Ill. 1

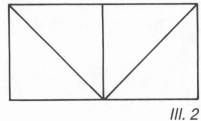

Ill. 2

5. Pin

6. Beginning in the upper right corner, line the edge of your presser foot with the marked line.

7. Sew ¼" seam on both sides of the diagonal lines. Do not backstitch. Ill. 3

*¼" seam allowance
15 stitches per inch*

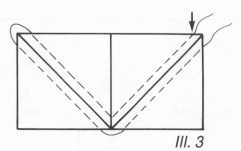

Ill. 3

8. Cut the blocks apart on the 6'' square lines. Cut apart on the diagonal lines. Ill. 1

Ill. 1

9. Stack in one stack.

10. Lay on the ironing board with the light side on the bottom. Fold back the dark triangle, and press the seam allowance toward the dark side.

11. Square up each piece to 5½''. Ill. 2   Be careful not to lose your points when trimming. Ill. 3.

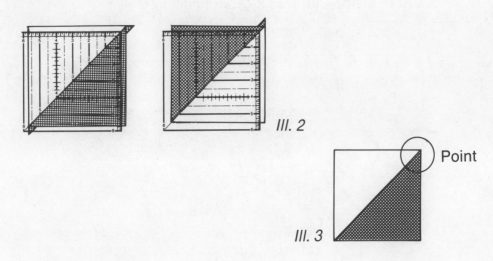

Ill. 2

Point

Ill. 3

Making the ⬜ :   These pieces must match the pieced triangles in length.

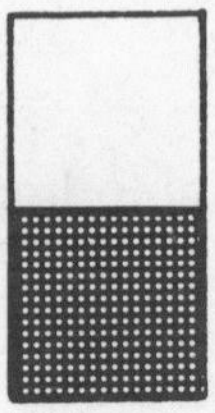

1. Place the 3⅛'' x 13'' light strip and the 3⅛'' x 13'' dark strip right sides together.

2. Press.

3. Seam together lengthwise. Ill. 1.

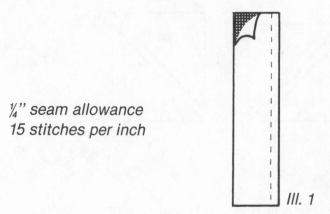

¼" seam allowance
15 stitches per inch

Ill. 1

4. Open up the strip. Press the seam toward the dark side.

5. Cut this strip into four 3⅛" sections. Ill. 2

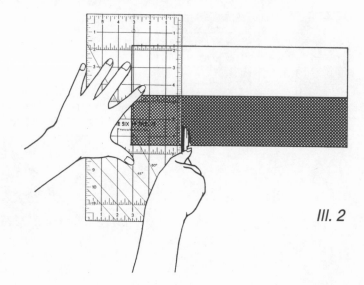

Ill. 2

Check:

The 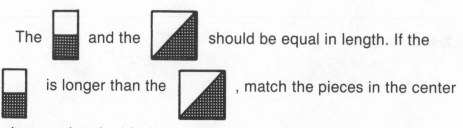 and the 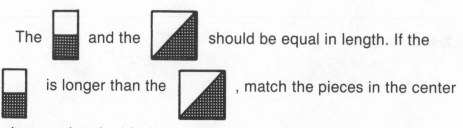 should be equal in length. If the 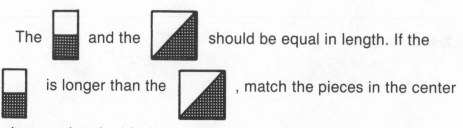 is longer than the 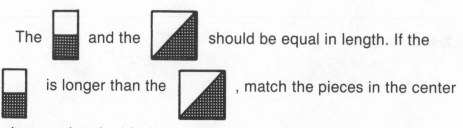 , match the pieces in the center when sewing the block together. Trim away the excess on the outside edge.

When sewing the next blocks, make an adjustment in the seam allowance when sewing the 3⅛" strips together.

Making the  **:**

1. Cut one 3⅛'' light square for the very center of the block.

Making the  **:**

1. Lay out the pieces following the illustration. Ill. 1

2. The numbers indicate the order the pieces are sewn together. Ill. 2

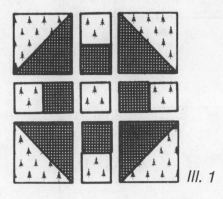

Ill. 1

1	2	7
3	4	8
5	6	9

Ill. 2

If the 's are longer than the 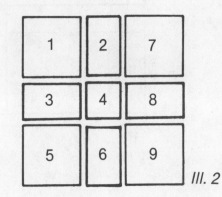 's, match them in the center and trim away the excess on the outside edge after the block is sewn together.

Now turn to page 91 for information on sewing one quilt block together.

Cutting Charts for Monkey Wrench

These charts give information on the sizes of fabric pieces to cut from your purchased yardage for the eight different sizes of quilts.

The quilts set together with the Monkey Wrench patchwork and the solid blocks take less time than those set together with lattice and cornerstones.

The following is an example of how to cut all pieces for the Crib Quilt on the opposite page. Ill. 1

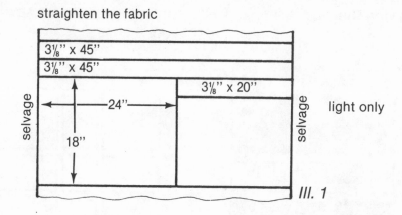

straighten the fabric

3⅛" x 45"
3⅛" x 45"
3⅛" x 20"
selvage
selvage
light only
24"
18"

Ill. 1

When you are cutting with the rotary cutter, the light and dark fabric can be layered right sides together and cut together at the same time. The fabric can even be folded in half and several thicknesses cut when doing the 3⅛" strips.

Once the pieces are cut, you can check them off in the space provided on the chart.

Cutting Charts for Monkey Wrench

Crib Quilt with Lattice and Cornerstones
Six Monkey Wrench

Cut . . . . To Make:

☐ two — 3⅛" x 45" strips light
☐ two — 3⅛" x 45" strips dark 24

☐ one — 3⅛" x 20" strip light 6   (3⅛" sq.)

☐ one — 18" x 24" light
☐ one — 18" x 24" dark 24

Crib Quilt with Patchwork and Solid Blocks
Five Monkey Wrench

Cut . . . . To Make:

☐ two — 3⅛" x 45" strips light
☐ two — 3⅛" x 45" strips dark 20

☐ one — 3⅛" x 17" strip light 5   (3⅛" sq.)

☐ one — 12" x 30" light
☐ one — 12" x 30" dark 20

☐ four medium solid blocks the same size as the
finished patchwork block

Cutting Charts for Monkey Wrench (cont.)

Lap Robe with Lattice and Cornerstones
Six Monkey Wrench

Cut . . . . **To Make:**

☐ two — 3⅛" x 45" strips light
☐ two — 3⅛" x 45" strips dark 24

☐ one — 3⅛" x 20" strip light . . . . 6 (3⅛" sq.)

☐ one — 18" x 24" light
☐ one — 18" x 24" dark 24

Lap Robe with Patchwork and Solid Blocks
Six Monkey Wrench

Cut . . . . **To Make:**

☐ two — 3⅛" x 45" strips light
☐ two — 3⅛" x 45" strips dark 24

☐ one — 3⅛" x 20" strip light . . . . 6 (3⅛" sq.)

☐ one — 18" x 24" light
☐ one — 18" x 24" dark 24

☐ six — medium solid blocks the same size as the
finished patchwork block

Cutting Charts for Monkey Wrench (cont.)

**Twin Quilt with Lattice Strips and Cornerstones
Fifteen Monkey Wrench**

Cut . . . . .To Make:

☐ five — 3⅛" x 45" strips light
☐ five — 3⅛" x 45" strips dark 60

☐ one — 3⅛" x 45" strip light
☐ one — 3⅛" x 8" strip light 15   (3⅛" sq.)

☐ two — 18" x 30" light
☐ two — 18" x 30" dark 60

**Twin Quilt with Patchwork and Solid Blocks
Nine Monkey Wrench**

Cut . . . . .To Make:

☐ three — 3⅛" x 45" strips light
☐ three — 3⅛" x 45" strips dark 36

☐ one — 3⅛" x 45" strip light 9   (3⅛" sq.)

☐ three — 12" x 18" light
☐ three — 12" x 18" dark 36

☐ nine — medium solid blocks the same size as the
finished patchwork block

40

Double-Queen Quilts with Lattice and Cornerstones
Twenty Monkey Wrench

Cut . . . . **To Make:**

☐ seven — 3⅛" x 45" strips light
☐ seven — 3⅛" x 45" strips dark 80

☐ one — 3⅛" x 45" strip light
☐ one — 3⅛" x 25" strip light 20   (3⅛" sq.)

☐ three — 12" x 24" light
☐ three — 12" x 24" dark

☐ three — 12" x 18" light
☐ three — 12" x 18" dark 80   4 extra for a pillow

Double-Queen Quilts with Patchwork and Solid Blocks
15 Monkey Wrench

Cut . . . . **To Make:**

☐ five — 3⅛" x 45" strips light
☐ five — 3⅛" x 45" strips dark 60

☐ one — 3⅛" x 45" strip light
☐ one — 3⅛" x 8" strip light 15   (3⅛" sq.)

☐ two — 18" x 30" light
☐ two — 18" x 30" dark 60

☐ fifteen — medium blocks the same size as the finished patchwork block

41

King Quilt with Lattice Strips and Cornerstones
25 Monkey Wrench

Cut . . . . .To Make:

☐ eight — 3⅛" x 45" strips light
☐ eight — 3⅛" x 45" strips dark 100

☐ two — 3⅛" x 45" strips light . . . . 25 (3⅛" sq.)

☐ four — 12" x 24" light
☐ four — 12" x 24" dark

☐ three — 12" x 18" light
☐ three — 12" x 18" dark 100

King Quilt with Patchwork and Solid Blocks
18 Monkey Wrench

Cut . . . . .To Make:

☐ six — 3⅛" x 45" strips light
☐ six — 3⅛" x 45" strips dark 72

☐ two — 3⅛" x 45" strips light . . . . 18 (3⅛" sq.)

☐ three — 12" x 24" light
☐ three — 12" x 24" dark

☐ two — 12" x 18" light
☐ two — 12" x 18" dark 72

☐ eighteen — medium solid blocks the same size as
the finished patchwork block

Multiple Assembly Sewing of the Monkey Wrench Block

Making the 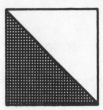 :

The drawings are a representation of technique only and may not be identical in size and shape to yours.

1. Following the individual Cutting Charts, prepare the exact number and sizes of light and dark larger squares and rectangles needed.

2. Place one light and one dark piece of the same size right sides together.

3. Press.

4. Draw on 6" square lines. Ill. 1

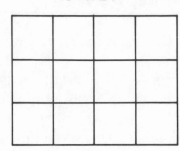

12" x 24"   *18" x 24"*

Ill. 1

5. Draw on diagonal lines every other row, beginning in the lower right corner. Ill. 2

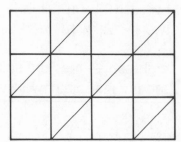

Ill. 2

6. Draw on diagonal lines in the opposite direction in the empty rows that are left. Ill. 1
Pin.

12" x 24"   *18" x 24"*

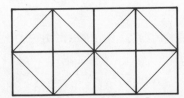 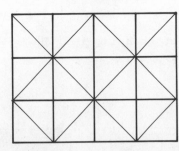

Ill. 1

7. Begin sewing in the upper right corner ¼" away from the diagonal line.

8. At the end of the first line, turn the strip and continue sewing ¼" from the diagonal line. Pivot the strip with the needle in the fabric.

9. Continuously sew, pivoting the fabric until you cannot sew any further. Turn the piece around. Ill. 2

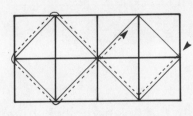 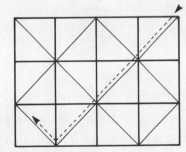

Ill. 2

10. Sew on the other side of the diagonal line. Ill. 3

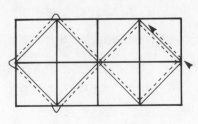 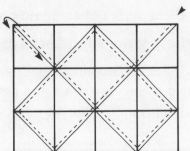

Ill. 3

44

11. Press

12. Cut apart on the 6'' square lines. Cut apart on the diagonal lines.

13. Press the seams to the dark side.

14. Square up to 5½''. Ill. 1   Be careful not to cut off the points while trimming. Ill. 2

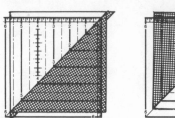 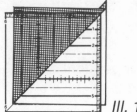 *Ill. 1*

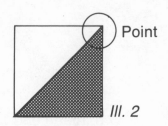

Point

Ill. 2

Making the  **:**

These pieces may be oversized. In the finished block, to match the pieced triangles in length, they may be trimmed. Use your serger and/or a magnetic seam guide in this step.

1. Following the individual Cutting Charts, prepare the exact number of 3⅛'' x 45'' light and dark strips.

2. Place a pair of light and dark strips right sides together.

3. Sew down only 3'' and stop. Press the seam to the dark side.

4. Place a pieced triangle next to this piece. Check to see that the two pieces are the same length. Make an adjustment in your seam allowance if they are not equal.

5. Continue seaming the pair together lengthwise. As soon as one pair is sewn, flashfeed and stitch all the remaining pairs. Ill. 1

¼" seam allowance
15 stitches per inch

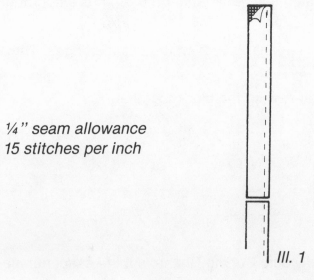

Ill. 1

6. Drop on the ironing board with the light on the bottom. Fold back the dark and press flat, pressing the seam to the dark side.

7. Stack as many as three sewn strips at a time in one pile on the cutting board. Ill. 2

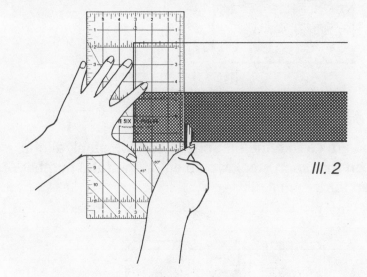

Ill. 2

8. Straighten the left edge.

9. Cut into 3⅛" sections.

10. Count out and stack the total number of needed.

Check:

It is important to match the center square. If 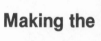 is longer than

the  , let the 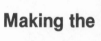 hang over on the outside edges. Trim

the outside edges after sewing the block together.

Making the ☐ :

1. Following the individual Cutting Charts, cut the exact number
of 3⅛'' light squares needed.

Making the 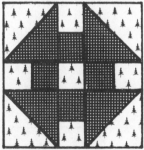 :

1. Lay out one block following the illustration.

2. Once you are certain the first one is correct, stack all the
other pieces on top. Each stack would equal the total number of
blocks needed for the quilt. Ill. 1

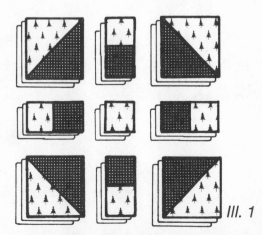

Ill. 1

3. The numbers indicate the order the pieces are sewn together. Ill. 2

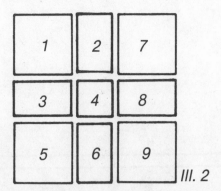

Ill. 2

4. Now turn to page 94 for information on multiple assembly sewing of the pieces together.

Check:

Match the center square. If hangs over on the outside

edges, trim the outside edges after sewing the block together.

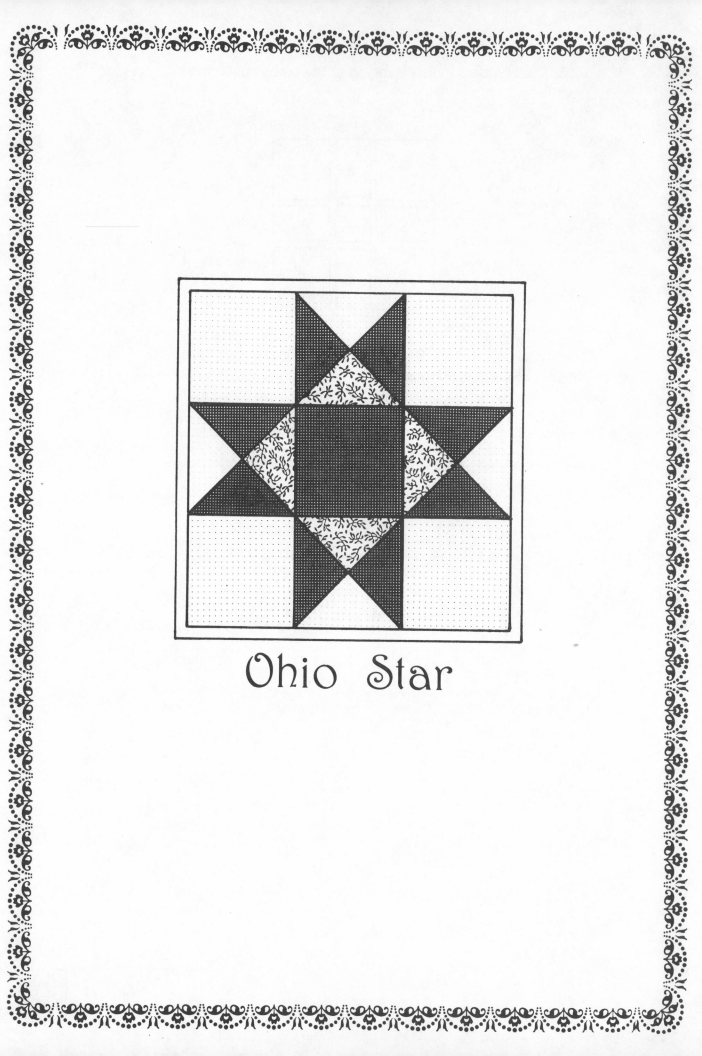

Ohio Star

Chapter 6

History

Stars easily lead the list for names of quilt patterns: Eight Point Star, Variable Star, Lone Star, Friendship Star, Twinkling Star, Morning Star, Feathered Star, and Star of Bethlehem to name only a few.

Even with the famous Ohio Star originating in the East, as the covered wagons rolled across the plains, so did the quilt pattern. It often showed up later under new names in various locations of the country.

Color Selection

The yardage charts and sewing directions are written for using the same light, medium, and dark throughout the quilt with newly purchased fabric. However, this is just a beginning for you. Apply your own individuality in color to add that wanted zest and excitement. Use the sample paste-up sheet to see how your block will look before you even start sewing.

The All-American look in a red, white, and blue star or the more modern version of beige, burgundy, and navy is always popular.

Try stacking bolts of these color combinations together in a fabric store. I always like to step back and "squint" at them together to see a blending of color.

light	medium	dark
beige	rust	navy blue
white	coral	green
cream	pink	purple
pink	burgundy	forest green

Color Variations

Use two different combinations of lights, mediums, and darks within one quilt. Divide the total yardage for the blocks by two, and alternate the blocks within the quilt.

For the following variations, divide the dark yardage by three. Purchase ⅓ for the center square, and ⅔'s for the points of the star.

Use a striped center square with the same stripe in the cornerstones or lattice strip.

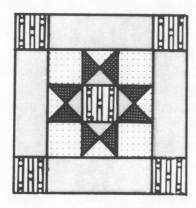

Cut one large flower or medallion from a large scaled print and use it in the center of each block.

Use two different darks within one block using a large scaled print and a small scaled print.

For a very contemporary look, use just lights and darks and alternate them for a positive-negative design. Using all solid Amish colors would certainly create a classic look.

Use a striped fabric in the triangles surrounding the center square.

2. Lay the longest side of the triangle parallel to the lines in the fabric. Mark and cut. Ill. 2

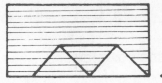

Ill. 2

1. Make a triangle template of ¼ of the 5½" square. Ill. 1

Ill. 1

3. Place the four triangles right sides together with the opposite fabric. Hold the fabric in place with two pieces of tape while you sew. Ill. 3

Ill. 3

Materials for One Ohio Star

Skill Level: Intermediate
Approximate Finished Size: 11½"
Approximate Construction Time: 45 minutes

Buy:

    ¼ yd. light calico

    ¼ yd. medium calico

    ¼ yd. dark calico

Cut . . . .**To Make :**

☐ one — 5½" square light
☐ one — 5½" square medium
☐ two — 5½" squares dark 4

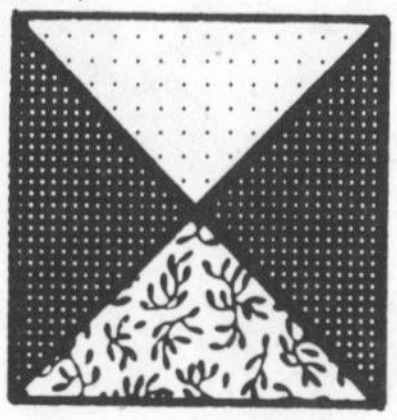

☐ one — 4½" square dark 1

☐ four — 4½" squares light 4

Once the pieces are cut, check them off in the box provided.

53

Sample Paste-Up Block — Paste in your fabric swatches

☐ light calico

☐ medium calico

☐ dark calico

☐ cornerstone

and

☐ lattice

or

☐ solid block

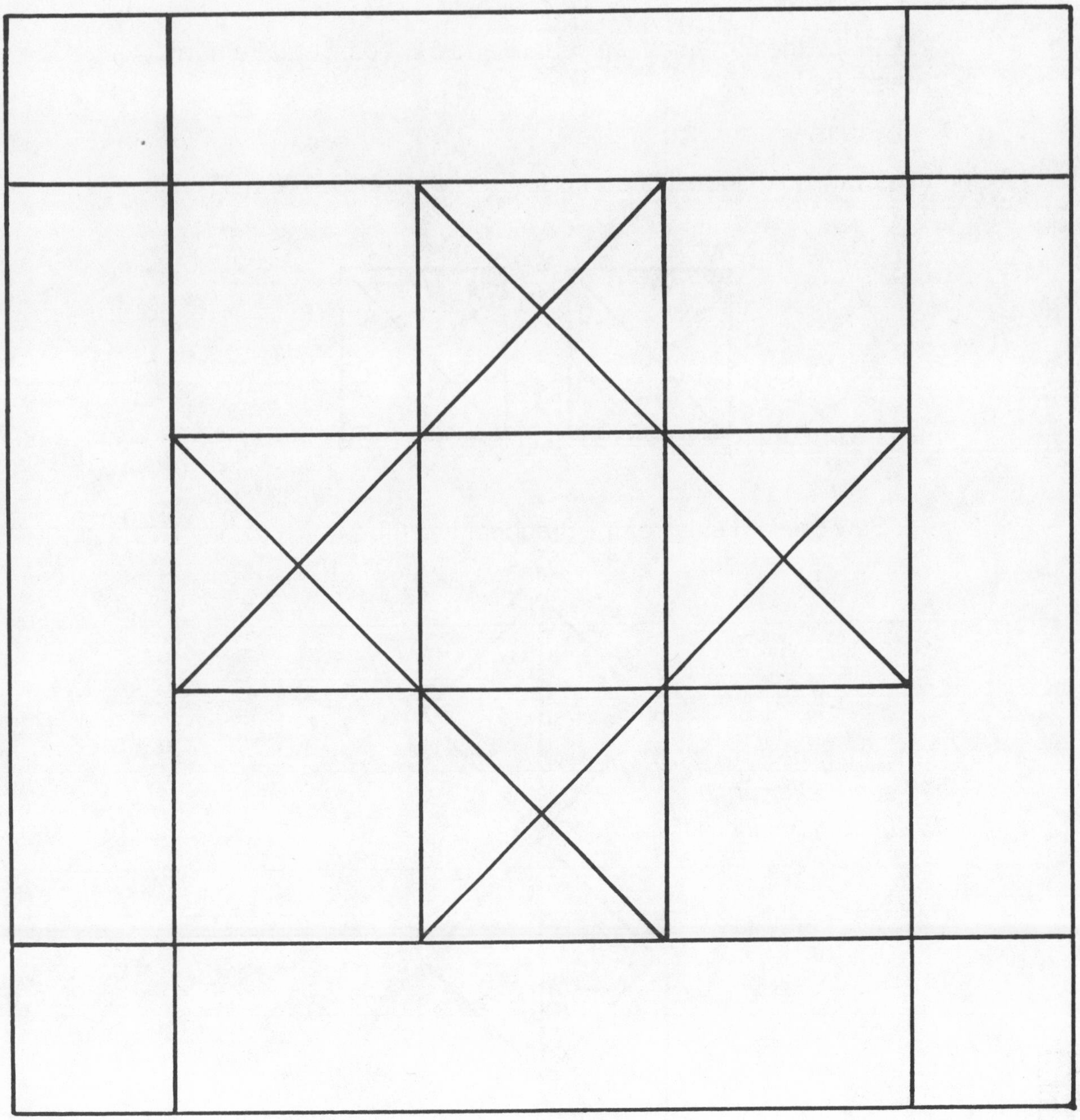

Sewing the Pieces for One Ohio Star

Making the :

1. Place the 5½" light square and the 5½" dark square right sides together.

2. Place the 5½" medium square and 5½" dark square right sides together.

3. Press.

4. Draw on diagonal lines. Ill. 1

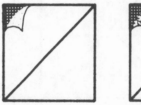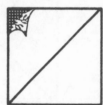

Ill. 1

5. Sew on both sides of the diagonal line. Ill. 2

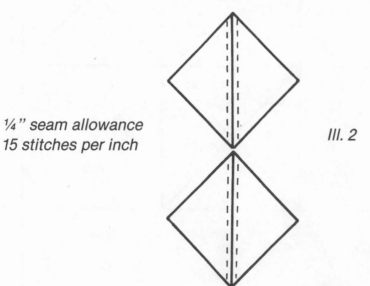

¼" seam allowance
15 stitches per inch

Ill. 2

6. With the rotary cutter and ruler, cut apart on the diagonals the opposite way. Ill. 1

Ill. 1

7. Cut apart on the marked diagonal lines. Ill. 2

Ill. 2

8. Press the seam allowance to the dark side.

9. Sort and stack the identical pieces into four equal piles. Ill. 3

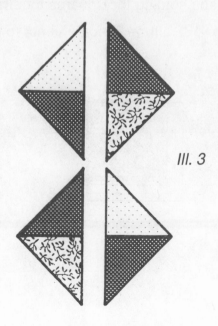

Ill. 3

Making the 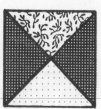 **:**

1. Place the first set right sides together. The seams have already been pressed toward the dark side and will lay flat. Match and finger pin the center.

2. Sew the triangles right sides together.

3. Flashfeed all sets. Ill. 1

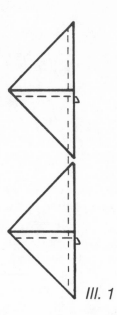

Ill. 1

4. Press the seams flat toward the dark/medium side.

5. Clip the threads holding the squares together.

6. Square up to 4½". Ill. 2   Be careful not to trim off the points. Ill. 3

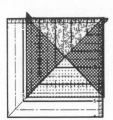 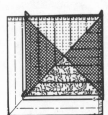 *Ill. 2*

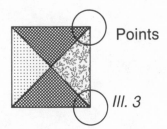

Points

Ill. 3

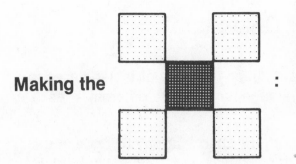

Making the 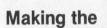 :

1. Cut the one 4½" dark square and the four 4½" light squares.

Making the  :

1. Lay out the pattern following the illustration. Ill. 1

2. The numbers indicate the order the pieces are sewn together. Ill. 2

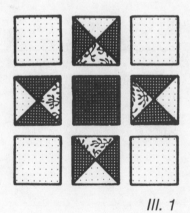

Ill. 1

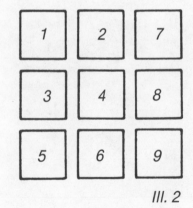

Ill. 2

3. Now turn to page 91 for information on sewing one quilt block together.

Cutting Charts for Ohio Star

These charts give information on the sizes of fabric pieces to cut from your purchased yardage for the eight different sizes of quilts.

The quilts set together with the Ohio Star patchwork and the solid blocks take less time than those set together with lattice and cornerstones.

The following is an example of how to cut all pieces for the Crib Quilt on the opposite page.

Light

straighten

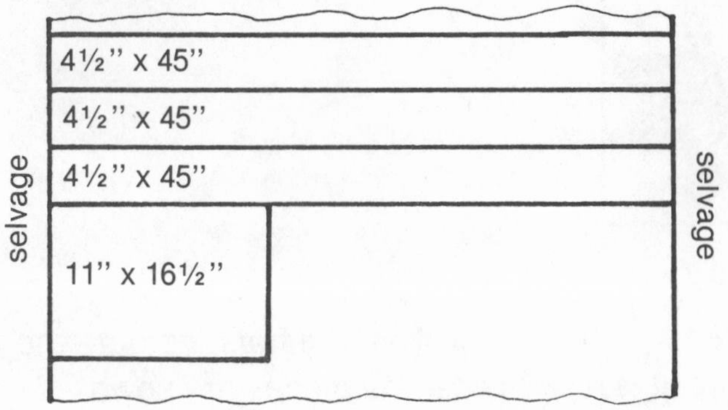

4½" x 45"
4½" x 45"
4½" x 45"
11" x 16½"
selvage
selvage

Medium

straighten

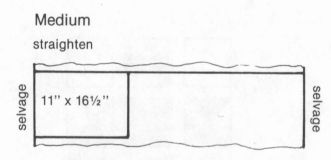

11" x 16½"
selvage
selvage

Dark

straighten

4½" x 45"
11" x 16½"
11" x 16½"
selvage
selvage

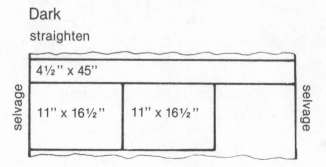

Once the pieces are cut, check them off in the box provided on the chart.

Cutting Charts for Ohio Star

Crib Quilt with Lattice and Cornerstone
6 Ohio Star

Cut.......................To Make:

☐ one — 11" x 16½" light calico
☐ one — 11" x 16½" dark calico .....12 ◿ 12 ◺

☐ one — 11" x 16½" medium calico
☐ one — 11" x 16½" dark calico .....12 ◿ 12 ◺

☐ one — 4½" x 45" dark calico ...... 6 ■ (4½")

☐ three — 4½" x 45" light calico .....24 ☐ (4½")

Crib Quilt with Patchwork and Solid Blocks
5 Ohio Star

Cut.......................To Make:

☐ one — 11" x 16½" light calico
☐ one — 11" x 16½" dark calico .....12 ◿ 12 ◺

☐ one — 11" x 16½" medium calico
☐ one — 11" x 16½" dark calico .....12 ◿ 12 ◺

☐ one — 4½" x 45" strip dark .... 6 ■ (4½")

☐ three — 4½" x 45" strips light .....24 ☐ (4½")

☐ four — medium solid blocks the same
size as the finished patchwork block

These measurements will yield one extra block.

Lap Robe with Lattice and Cornerstones
6 Ohio Star

Cut . . . . To Make:

☐ one — 11" x 16½" light calico
☐ one — 11" x 16½" dark calico 12   12

☐ one — 11" x 16½" medium calico
☐ one — 11" x 16½" dark calico 12   12

☐ one — 4½" x 45" dark calico 6   (4½")

☐ three — 4½" x 45" light calico 24   (4½")

Lap Robe with Patchwork and Solid Blocks
6 Ohio Star

Cut . . . . To Make:

☐ one — 11" x 16½" light calico
☐ one — 11" x 16½" dark calico 12   12

☐ one — 11" x 16½" medium calico
☐ one — 11" x 16½" dark calico 12   12

☐ one — 4½" x 45" dark calico 6   (4½")

☐ three — 4½" x 45" light calico 24   (4½")

☐ six — solid blocks the same size as
the finished patchwork block

Cutting Charts for Ohio Star (continued)

Twin Quilt with Lattice Strips and Cornerstones
15 Ohio Star

Cut . . . . .To Make:

☐ one — 16½" x 27½" light calico
☐ one — 16½" x 27½" dark calico . . .30   30

☐ one — 16½" x 27½" medium calico
☐ one — 16½" x 27½" dark calico . . .30   30

☐ two — 4½" x 45" dark calico 15   (4½")

☐ seven — 4½" x 45" light calico 60   (4½")

Twin Quilt with Patchwork and Solid Blocks
9 Ohio Star

Cut . . . . .To Make:

☐ one — 16½" x 16½" light calico
☐ one — 16½" x 16½" dark calico 18   18

☐ one — 16½" x 16½" medium calico
☐ one — 16½" x 16½" dark calico . . .18   18

☐ one — 4½" x 45" dark calico 9   (4½")

☐ four — 4½" x 45" light calico 36   (4½")

☐ nine — medium solid blocks the same
size as the finished patchwork block

62

Double-Queen Quilts with Lattice and Cornerstones
20 Ohio Star

Cut . . . . To Make:

☐ one — 22" x 27½" light calico
☐ one — 22" x 27½" dark calico 40   40

☐ one — 22" x 27½" medium calico
☐ one — 22" x 27½" dark calico 40   40

☐ three — 4½" x 45" dark calico 20   (4½")

☐ nine — 4½" x 45" light calico 80   (4½")

Double-Queen Quilts with Patchwork and Solid Blocks
15 Ohio Star

Cut . . . . To Make:

☐ one — 16½" x 27½" light calico
☐ one — 16½" x 27½" dark calico . . . 30   30

☐ one — 16½" x 27½" medium calico
☐ one — 16½" x 27½" dark calico . . . 30   30

☐ two — 4½" x 45" dark calico 15   (4½")

☐ seven — 4½" x 45" light calico 60   (4½")

☐ fifteen — medium solid blocks the
same size as the finished patchwork
block

King Quilt with Lattice and Cornerstones
25 Ohio Star

Cut . . . . To Make:

☐ one — 27½" x 27½" light calico
☐ one — 27½" x 27½" dark calico . . .50 ◸   50 ◺

☐ one — 27½" x 27½" medium calico
☐ one — 27½" x 27½" dark calico . . .50 ◸   50 ◺

☐ three — 4½" x 45" dark calico . . . . .25 ◼ (4½")

☐ twelve — 4½" x 45" light calico . . .100 ◻ (4½")

King Quilt with Patchwork and Solid Blocks
18 Ohio Star

Cut . . . . To Make:

☐ one — 16½" x 33" light calico
☐ one — 16½" x 33" dark calico . . . . .36 ◸   36 ◺

☐ one — 16½" x 33" medium calico
☐ one — 16½" x 33" dark calico . . . . .36 ◸   36 ◺

☐ two — 4½" x 45" dark calico . . . . . .18 ◼ (4½")

☐ eight — 4½" x 45" light calico . . . . .72 ◻ (4½")

☐ eighteen — medium solid blocks the
same size as the finished patchwork
block

Multiple Assembly Sewing of the Ohio Star

Making the 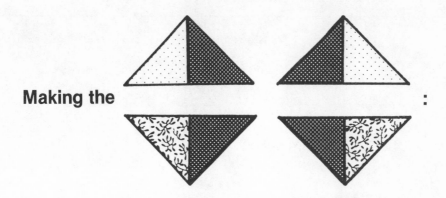 :

1. Following the individual Cutting Charts, prepare the exact number of larger light, medium, and dark squares or rectangles needed.

2. Place a piece of light and a piece of dark the same size right sides together.

3. Place a piece of medium and a piece of dark the same size right sides together.

4. Press them right sides together.

5. Draw on 5½'' square lines, using the gridded cutting board and 6'' x 24'' ruler. Ill. 1

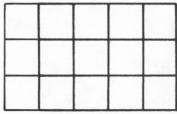

16½'' x 27½''   Ill. 1

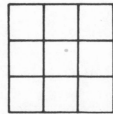

16½'' x 16½''

This drawing represents technique only. These pieces may not be identical to yours depending on your size quilt.

6. Draw on diagonal lines. Ill. 1

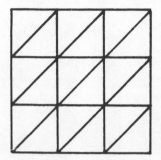

Ill. 1

7. Pin the two pieces together at the corners and several times in the center. Ill. 2

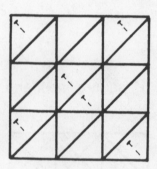

Ill. 2

8. Sew on both sides of the diagonal line. Ill. 3

¼" seam allowance
15 stitches per inch
Do not backstitch.

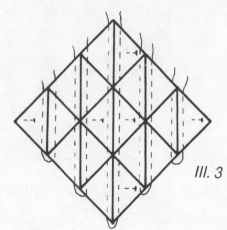

Ill. 3

9. Remove the pins and press.

10. With the piece laying flat on the cutting board, cut on the diagonal the opposite way with the rotary cutter and ruler. Ill. 1

Keep the pieces from spreading apart.

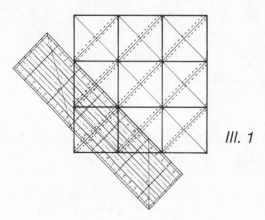

Ill. 1

11. Cut apart on the 5½'' square lines, and the diagonal lines. Ill. 2

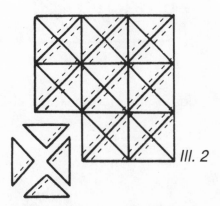

Ill. 2

12. Stack in one stack with the dark on the top of the stack.

13. Drop them on the ironing board with the light on the bottom.

14. A few threads may be sewn across the tips of the blocks. These come out easily as you open and press. As you open them with your left hand, press the seams to the dark side with the iron in your right hand. Ill. 1

Ill. 1

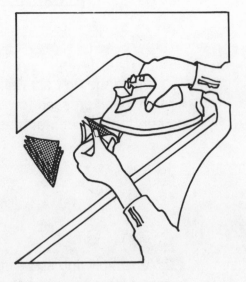

15. Sort and stack the identical pieces into four equal piles as you press. Ill. 2

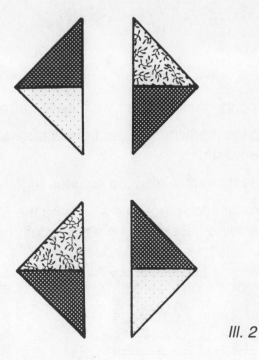

Ill. 2

Making the 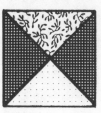 **:**

1. Place the first set right sides together. The seams have already been pressed toward the dark side and will lay flat. Make certain that the center matches.

2. Assembly line sew the triangles right sides together. Ill. 1

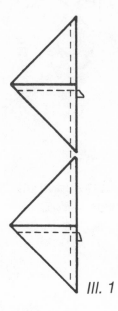

Ill. 1

3. Drop on the ironing board with the light/dark on the bottom.

4. Lift up the medium/dark, and press the seams flat behind the medium/dark side.

5. Clip the threads joining the squares together.

6. Square up each piece to 4½'', using the 6'' square ruler and rotary cutter. Ill. 2   Be careful not to trim off the points. Ill. 3

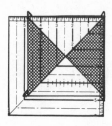 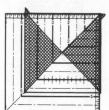

Ill. 2

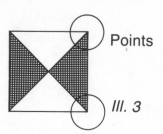

Points

Ill. 3

Making the 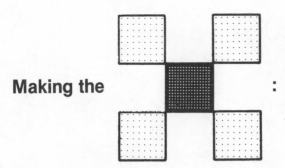 **:**

1. Check the individual Cutting Charts for the exact number of 4½'' x 45'' strips and 4½'' squares of the light and dark.

2. Stack up several strips on top of each other.

3. Layer cut all the 4½'' squares.

Making the 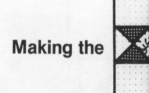 **:**

1. Lay out one block following the illustration.

2. Once you are certain the first one is correct, stack all the other pieces on top. Each stack would equal the total number of blocks needed for the quilt. Ill. 1

3. The numbers indicate the order the pieces are sewn together. Ill. 2

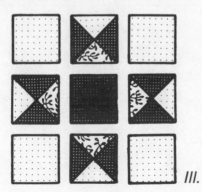

Ill. 1

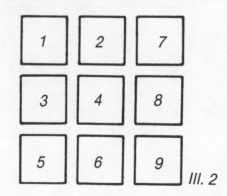

Ill. 2

4. Now turn to page 94 for information on the multiple assembly sewing of blocks together.

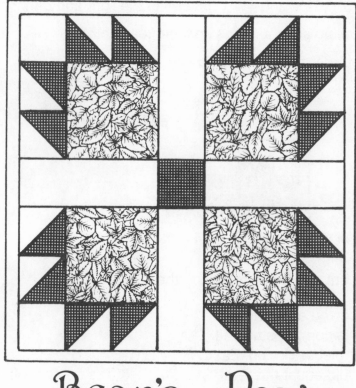

Bear's Paw

Chapter 7

History

The name Bear's Paw reflects the dangers encountered on the frontier. In more settled areas, once the bears had moved on, the same pattern was often called Duck's Foot in the Mud. The Pennsylvania Friends called it Hand of Friendship.

Bears Paw, the most advanced pattern in this book, is not particularly difficult, but time consuming. The "claw" pieces are small but the final effect is well worth it.

Color Selection

The yardage charts and sewing directions are written for using the same light, medium, and dark throughout the quilt with newly purchased fabric. However, using a variety of lights, mediums, and darks may add just the excitement you want to your quilt.

It sure is easy to miss those few corners that don't quite match in a quilt that is alive and vibrant with color.

I prefer using a very deep medium calico printed in a large scale for the paw, with a small scaled dark print for the claws. A minidot appears as a solid and helps to break down a busy look. Consider the dot for the narrow strips between the paws.

Play with these colors and paste them up on the sample block to see how they look together.

light	medium	dark
rose	gray	burgundy
gold	rust	brown
beige	burgundy	navy
beige	blue	brown

These colors are just suggestions. The fun is all yours!

Color Variations

Use two different combinations of lights, mediums, and darks within one quilt. Divide the total yardage for the blocks by two, and alternate the blocks within the quilt.

Use a single flower or medallion in the center square. Repeat it in the cornerstones.

Reverse the dark with the light. Use a medium for the strips in between the paws.

Use a second light for the strips.

Use a medallion, large print or stripe in the four large squares.

You can figure your yardage for any of the variations by referring to the Cutting Charts, pages 78-82. See how much you need for your particular piece in your specific quilt size.

For a very feminine look, turn the Bear's Paw into a Rosebud just with the use of color.

Use all solids for a contemporary look.

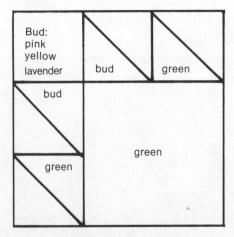

Bud:
pink
yellow
lavender

bud

green

bud

green

green

Use a large scale striped fabric in the four largest squares.

To cut out your pieces on the stripe, lay your template with opposite corners touching the line. Ill. 1

Ill. 1

When making the , lay out your squares with all the stripes turning the same direction. Ill. 2.

Ill. 2

You create a very exciting look when you use other stripes from the print in the center square, cornerstones, and borders.

Materials for One Bear's Paw

Skill Level: Advanced
Approximate Finished Size: 13"
Approximate Construction Time: 1 hour

Buy:

¼ yd. light calico
¼ yd. medium calico
¼ yd. dark calico

Cut.....................................To Make:

☐ one — 6" x 12" light

☐ one — 6" x 12" dark.........................16 ◸

☐ one — 2½" x 11" strip ....4 ☐

☐ four — 4½" squares medium ....4 ▨

☐ four — 2½" x 6½" light ....4 ▭

☐ one — 2½" square dark ....1 ■

Once the pieces are cut, you can check them off in the space
provided on the chart.

75

Sample Paste-Up Block — Paste in your fabric swatches.

□ light calico

□ medium calico

□ dark calico

□ cornerstone

and

□ lattice

or

□ solid block

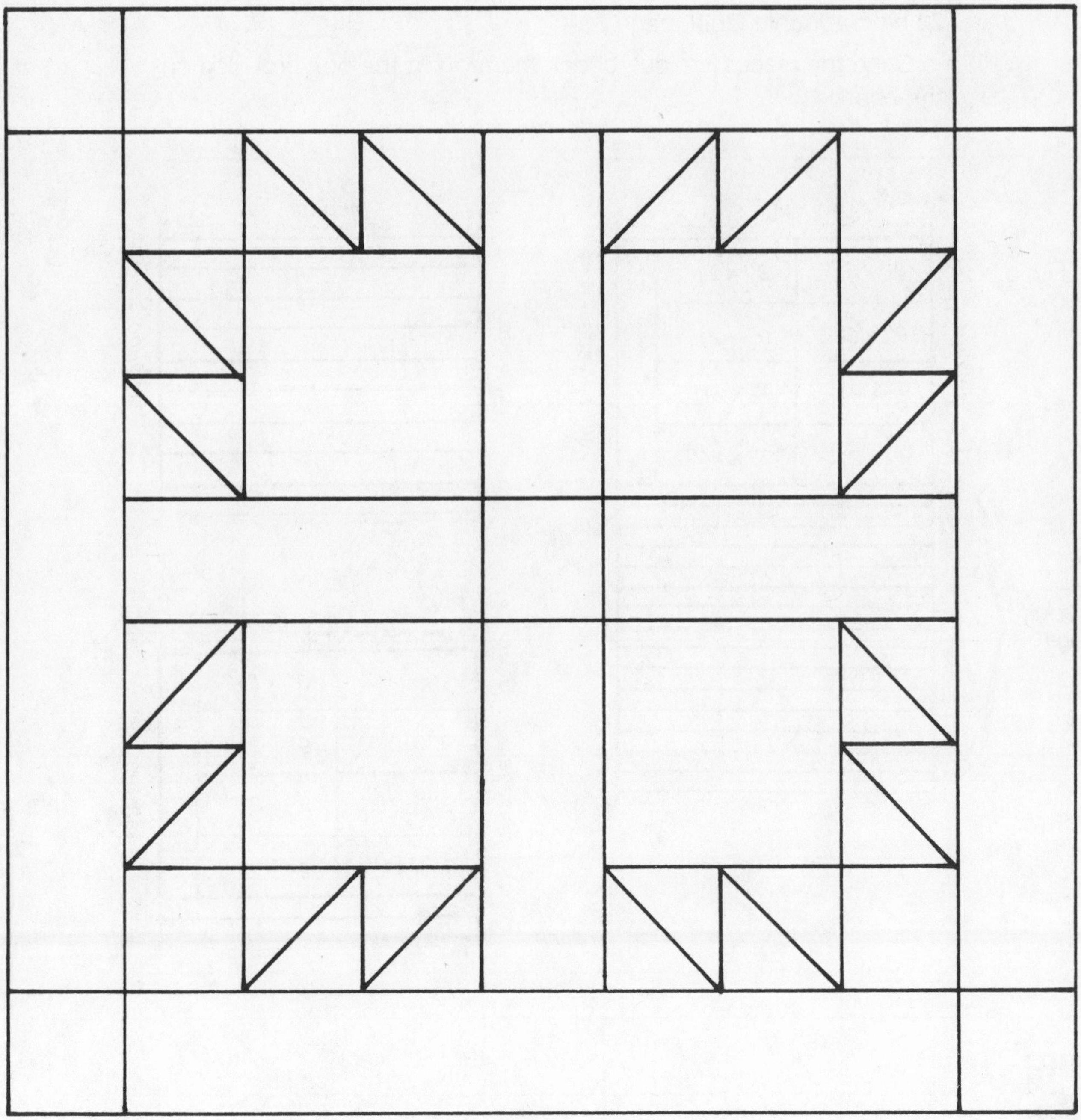

Cutting Charts for Bear's Paw

These charts give information on the sizes of fabric pieces to cut from your purchased yardage for the eight different sizes of quilts.

The Bear's Paw when finished is larger than the other patterns. For that reason, as you are sewing your blocks, lay them out on your bed and see how they fit. You may not need to make as many blocks as originally planned. This pattern definitely takes more fabric lost to the seam allowance, more sewing time, and more patience in matching pieces, but the finished quilt is well worth the effort.

The following is an example of how to cut all pieces for the 20 block Double Quilt, page 81.

Once the pieces are cut, check them off in the box provided on the chart.

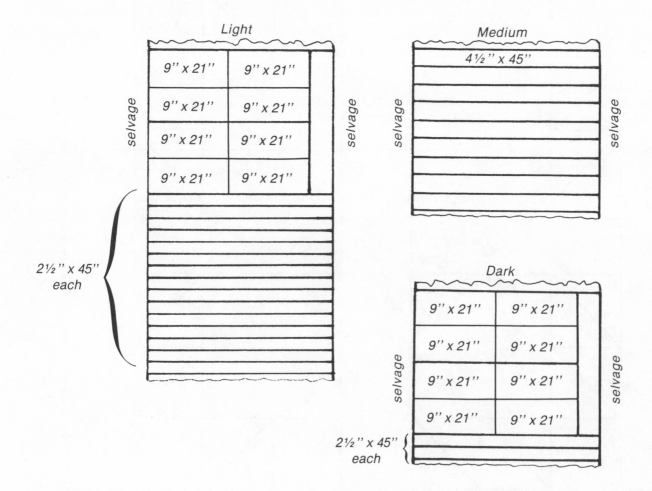

Cutting Charts for Bear's Paw

Crib Quilt with Lattice and Cornerstones   6 Bear's Paw

Cut . . . . To Make:

☐ two — 9" x 24" light calico
☐ two — 9" x 24" dark calico 96

☐ two — 2½" x 45" strips light 24

☐ three — 4½" x 45" strips medium 24

☐ four — 2½" x 45" strips light 24

☐ one — 2½" x 15" strip dark 6

Crib Quilt with Patchwork and Solid Blocks   5 Bear's Paw

Cut . . . . To Make:

☐ two — 9" x 21" light calico
☐ two — 9" x 21" dark calico 80

☐ two — 2½" x 45" strips light 20

☐ three — 4½" x 45" strips medium 20

☐ four — 2½" x 45" strips light 20

☐ one — 2½" x 13" strip dark 5

☐ four — medium solid blocks the same size as the finished patchwork blocks.

Cutting Charts for Bear's Paw (continued)

Lap Robe with Lattice and Cornerstones   6 Bear's Paw

Cut .... **To Make:**

☐ two — 9" x 24" light calico
☐ two — 9" x 24" dark calico 96   ◨

☐ two — 2½" x 45" strips light 24   ☐

☐ three — 4½" x 45" strips medium 24   ▦

☐ four — 2½" x 45" strips light 24   ▭

☐ one — 2½" x 15" strip dark 6   ■

Lap Robe with Patchwork and Solid Blocks   6 Bear's Paw

Cut .... **To Make:**

☐ two — 9" x 24" light calico
☐ two — 9" x 24" dark calico 96   ◨

☐ two — 2½" x 45" strips light 24   ☐

☐ three — 4½" x 45" strips medium 24   ▦

☐ four — 2½" x 45" strips light 24   ▭

☐ one — 2½" x 15" strip dark 6   ■

☐ six — medium solid blocks the same size as the finished patchwork blocks

Cutting Charts for Bear's Paw (continued)

Twin Quilt with Lattice and Cornerstones   15 Bear's Paw

Cut . . . . To Make:

☐ six — 9'' x 21'' light calico
☐ six — 9'' x 21'' dark calico 240   (12 extra)

☐ four — 2½'' x 45'' strips light 60

☐ seven — 4½'' x 45'' strips medium 60

☐ ten — 2½'' x 45'' strips light 60

☐ one — 2½'' x 45'' strip dark 15

Twin Quilt with Patchwork and Solid Blocks 9 Bear's Paw

Cut . . . . To Make:

☐ three — 9'' x 21'' light calico
☐ three — 9'' x 21'' dark calico

☐ one — 9'' x 12'' light calico
☐ one — 9'' x 12'' dark calico 144   (6 extra)

☐ three — 2½'' x 45'' strips light 36

☐ four — 4½'' x 45'' strips medium 36

☐ six — 2½'' x 45'' strips light 36

☐ one — 2½'' x 23'' strip dark   9

☐ nine — medium solid blocks the same size as the finished
   patchwork blocks

Cutting Charts for Bear's Paw (continued)

Double-Queen Quilts w/ Lattice & Cornerstones   20 Bear's Paw

Cut	To Make:		
☐ eight — 9" x 21" light calico			
☐ eight — 9" x 21" dark calico	320	◩	(16 extra for pillow)
☐ five — 2½" x 45" strips light	80	☐	
☐ nine — 4½" x 45" strips medium	80	▨	
☐ ten — 2½" x 45" strips light	80	▭	
☐ two — 2½" x 45" strips dark	20	■	

If you just want a coverlet size quilt for a double bed, you may only need to make 15 blocks as in the twin size quilt.

Dbl-Queen Quilts w/ Patchwork & Solid Blocks   15 Bear's Paw

Cut	To Make:		
☐ six — 9" x 21" light calico			
☐ six — 9" x 21" dark calico	240	◩	(12 extra)
☐ four — 2½" x 45" strips light	60	☐	
☐ seven — 4½" x 45" strips medium	60	▨	
☐ ten — 2½" x 45" strips light	60	▭	
☐ one — 2½" x 45" strip dark	15	■	
☐ fifteen — medium solid blocks the same size as the finished patchwork blocks			

Cutting Charts for Bear's Paw (continued)

King Quilt w/ Lattice Strips & Cornerstones 25 Bear's Paw

Cut . . . . .To Make:

- ☐ nine — 9" x 21" light calico
- ☐ nine — 9" x 21" dark calico

- ☐ one — 9" x 12" light calico
- ☐ one — 9" x 12" dark calico 400   (2 extra)

- ☐ six — 2½" x 45" strips light 100

- ☐ twelve — 4½" x 45" strips medium 100

- ☐ seventeen — 2½" x 45" strips light . . .100

- ☐ two — 2½" x 45" strips dark 25

King Quilt with Patchwork & Solid Blocks   18 Bear's Paw

Cut . . . . .To Make:

- ☐ seven — 9" x 21" light calico
- ☐ seven — 9" x 21" dark calico 288   (6 extra)

- ☐ five — 2½" x 45" strips light 72

- ☐ eight — 4½" x 45" strips medium 72

- ☐ twelve — 2½" x 45" strips light 72

- ☐ one — 2½" x 45" strip dark
- ☐ one — 2¼" square 18

- ☐ eighteen — medium solid blocks the same size as the finished patchwork blocks

Sewing the Pieces for Bear's Paw — One Block or Multiple Assembly

The technique for sewing one Bear's Paw or many Bear's Paw is the same.

Making the :

1. Following the individual Cutting Charts, prepare the exact number and sizes of light and dark larger squares or rectangles needed.

2. Place a light and a dark square or rectangle of the same size right sides together. Press.

3. Draw on 3" square lines, using your gridded cutting board and 6" x 24" ruler. Ill. 1

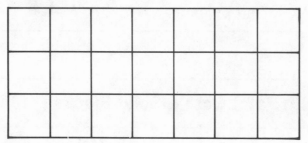

Ill. 1

4. Draw on diagonal lines every other row, beginning in the lower right corner. Ill. 2

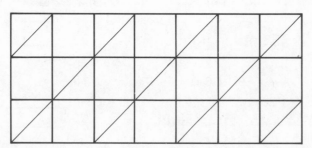

Ill. 2

5. Draw on diagonal lines in the opposite direction in the empty rows that are left. Ill. 3

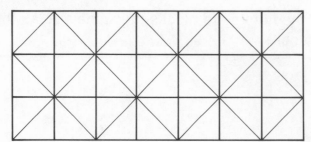

Ill. 3

83

6. Pin the two pieces together in the center of the diamonds.

7. Begin sewing in the upper right corner ¼'' away from the diagonal line.

8. At the end of the first line, turn the strip and continue sewing ¼'' from the diagonal line. Pivot the strip with the needle in the fabric at the 3'' grid lines. Ill. 1

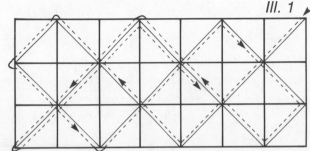

Ill. 1

9. Continuously sew, pivoting the fabric until you reach the left-hand corner and cannot sew any further. Turn the piece around.

10. Sew on the other side of the diagonal line. Do not backstitch. Ill. 2

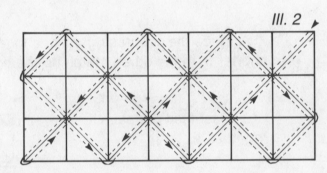

Ill. 2

11. Press.

12. Lay on top of the cutting board. With the rotary cutter and 6'' x 24'' ruler, cut apart on the 3'' square lines. Cut apart on all the diagonal lines exactly as you marked them. Ill. 3

Ill. 3

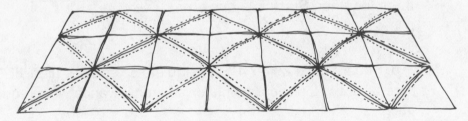

13. Press the seam toward the dark side.

14. Stack all the into four equal stacks.

Making the 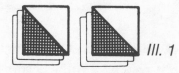 **:**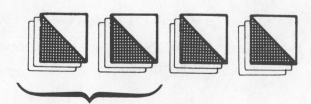

Only half of the  will be used in this step.

1. Lay out two stacks in this order next to the sewing machine. Ill. 1

Ill. 1

2. Place the squares right sides together. If one square is shorter than the other, match up the bottom edges.

3. Flashfeed the pairs together. Ill. 2

4. Lay the long chain of pieces on the ironing board. Fold back each block and press.

Ill. 2

5. Clip the threads holding them together. Stack into one pile.

6. Square up to 2½'' x 4½'', using the 6'' square ruler. Ill. 3   Be careful not to lose your points or seam allowance when squaring up. Ill. 4

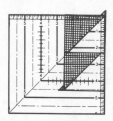 

Ill. 3

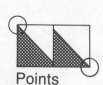

Points

Ill. 4

Making the :

    1. Following the individual Cutting Charts, prepare the exact number of 4½'' medium squares needed.

    2. Stack into one pile.

Making the  :

    1. Lay the two piles out next to your sewing machine in this order. Ill. 1

Ill. 1

    2. Place them right sides together.

    3. Flashfeed all pairs together. The illustration shows how to lay the seams flat. Ill. 2

    4. Press the seams to lay behind the 4½'' squares.

    5. Clip the threads that connect them together.

    6. Stack into one pile.

Ill. 2

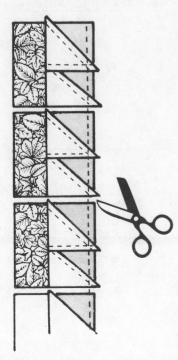

Making the  :

1. Following the individual Cutting Charts, prepare the exact number of 2½" light strips needed.

Making the  :

1. Lay this pattern out next to the sewing machine. Ill. 1

Ill. 1

2. Flashfeed together all the .

3. Square up to 2½" x 4½". Be careful not to lose your points or seam allowance when trimming. Ill. 2

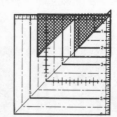

Ill. 2

4. Turn the pieces to the wrong side and upside down. With the 2½" light strip right side up, flashfeed on the pieces. Ill. 3

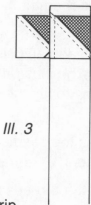

Ill. 3

5. Press the seams away from the light strip.

6. Cut the 2½" strip apart.

7. Stack in one pile.

Making the  :

1. Lay out these two stacks in this pattern next to the sewing machine. Ill. 1

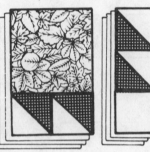

Ill. 1

2. Place these pieces right sides together. Pin and match the point indicated by the arrow. Ill. 2

Ill. 2

3. Flashfeed together. From the illustration, note the way the seams lay flat. Ill. 3. Press.

4. Clip the threads holding them together.

5. Stack them into four equal piles.

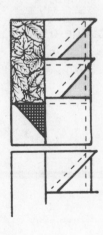

Ill. 3

Making the **:**

1. Following the individual Cutting Charts, cut the exact number of 2½'' dark squares needed.

2. Stack them into one pile.

Making the  **:**

1. The length of the 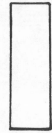 and the  should

be equal. Most sewers find that a 2½''x 6½'' strip is perfect for them. However, this depends on each individual's sewing techniques. Check to find out what length is best to fit into your block.

2. Following the individual Cutting Charts, prepare the exact number of 2½'' strips times the length of the paw.

3. Stack them into four equal piles.

Making the  **:**

1. Lay out one block following the above illustration. *(If you are only making one block, disregard step 2.)*

2. Once you are certain the first one is correct, stack all the other pieces on top. Each stack would equal the total number of blocks needed for the quilt. Ill. 1

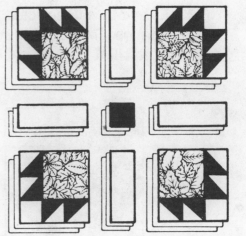

Ill. 1

3. The numbers indicate the order the pieces are sewn together. Ill. 2

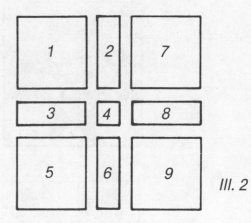

Ill. 2

4. Now turn to page 91 for information on sewing one block together, or to page 94 for information on the multiple assembly sewing of blocks together.

Chapter 8

Sewing the Pieces into One Block

Step 1 may have already been completed.

1. Lay out your selected pattern following the matching illustration. The numbers indicate the order the pieces are sewn together. Ill. 1

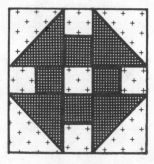

1	2	7
3	4	8
5	6	9

1	2	7
3	4	8
5	6	9

1	2	7
3	4	8
5	6	9

Ill. 1

Sewing the First Two Vertical Rows

1. Start in the upper left hand corner. Pick up piece #2 and flip it right sides together onto #1.

2. Stitch down about ½" to anchor the two together. Fingerpin the opposite corner and stretch the two to meet. Stitch. *Do not cut the threads or lift the pressure foot.*

3. Pick up pieces #3 and #4. Butt them right behind the first two.

4. Anchor the two with ½" of stitching. Fingerpin the corners as before. Stretch the two to meet. Stitch.

5. Continue butting on #5 and #6 in the same manner. Ill. 1

Do not cut the pieces apart.

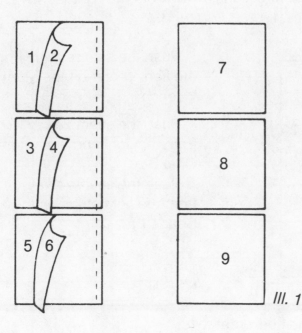

The pieces in your layout may vary in shape from the illustration depending on your choice of pattern.

Ill. 1

Sewing the Third Vertical Row

1. Place #7 right sides together onto #2.

2. Stretch and stitch the two to meet. Ill. 1

3. Butt, stretch, and stitch #8 onto #4.

4. Butt, stretch and stitch #9 onto #6.

Do not cut the pieces apart.

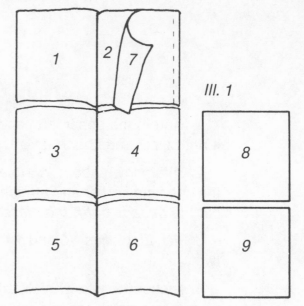

Ill. 1

Sewing the Horizontal Rows

1. Flip the top row down onto the second row with right sides together.

2. Stretch and stitch the pieces to meet. Where the two pieces are joined by a thread, match the seam carefully. Push the seam allowances in opposite directions, away from the light fabrics and toward the dark fabrics. Ill. 2

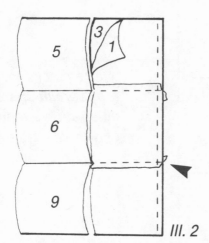

Ill. 2

Push the seams away from the light center on the Monkey Wrench.

Push the seams away from the light corners on the Ohio Star.

Push the seams away from the light strips on the Bear's Paw.

3. Stitch the second horizontal row.

Chapter 9

Multiple Assembly Sewing of the Pieces into Blocks

Stacking Your Pieces

Steps 1 and 2 may have already been completed.

1. Lay out your selected pattern following the matching illustration. The numbers indicate the order the pieces are sewn together. Ill. 1

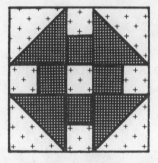

1	2	7
3	4	8
5	6	9

1	2	7
3	4	8
5	6	9

1	2	7
3	4	8
5	6	9

Ill. 1

2. Stack all the identical pieces on top of the first following the pattern. Stack up as many blocks as you need for your quilt. Ill. 1

The pieces in your layout may vary in shape from the illustration depending on your choice of pattern.

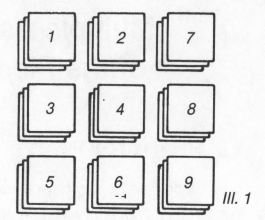

Ill. 1

3. Place a pin at the bottom of every #6 piece. This will indicate the end of the row in each block in the following steps.

4. Lay a ruler over the third row. This is to remind you that you are not ready to use these pieces yet.

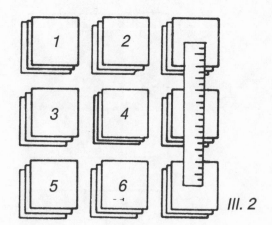

Ill. 2

5. Start in the upper left hand corner. Pick up piece #2 and flip it right sides together onto #1. Pick up #4 and flip it right sides together onto #3. Pick up #6 and flip it right sides together onto #5. Ill. 1

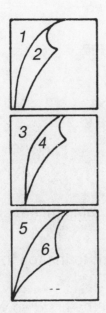 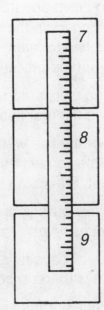

III. 1

Sewing the First Two Vertical Rows

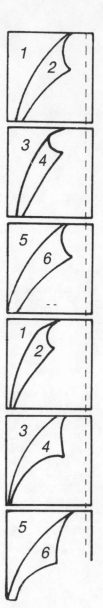

1. Start in the upper left hand corner. Pick up pieces #1 and #2.

2. Stitch down about ½" to anchor the two together. Finger pin the other corner and stretch the two to meet. Stitch. *Do not cut the threads or lift the pressure foot.*

3. Pick up pieces #3 and #4. Butt them right behind the first two.

4. Anchor the two with ½" of stitching. Fingerpin the corners as before. Stretch the two to meet. Stitch.

5. Continue butting on #5 and #6 in the same manner. *Do not cut the pieces apart.*

6. Once you have finished this step, return to the top to #1 and #2. Repeat with the second block.

7. Continue butting and stitching until all the first two vertical rows of all the blocks are sewn.

8. To organize the pieces into one compact pile, accordion fold the pieces starting at the end where you just finished sewing.

Sewing the Third Vertical Row

Remove the ruler.

1. Place #7 right sides together onto #2.

2. Stretch and stitch the two to meet. Ill. 1

3. Butt, stretch, and stitch #8 onto #4.

4. Butt, stretch and stitch #9 onto #6.

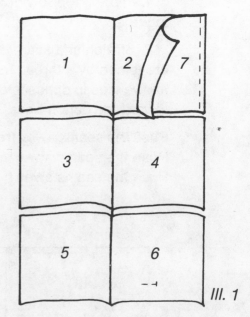

Ill. 1

The pin on #6 indicates you have finished the first block. Do not cut the threads holding the pieces together.

5. Return to #7 of the next block and repeat the sewing process until the third vertical row on all the blocks are stitched. Ill. 2

6. Snip the threads holding the blocks together every third row. The pin in #6 will help indicate this.

7. Stack all the blocks into one pile.

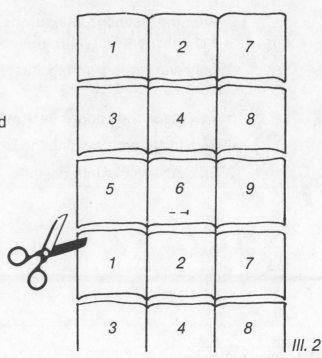

Ill. 2

Sewing the Horizontal Rows

1. Flip the top row down onto the second row with right sides together.

2. Stretch and stitch the pieces to meet. Where the two pieces are joined by a thread, match the seam carefully. Push the seam allowances in opposite directions, away from the light fabrics and toward the dark fabrics. Ill. 1

Push the seams away from the light center on the Monkey Wrench. Push the seams away from the light corners on the Ohio Star. Push the seams away from the light strips on the Bear's Paw.

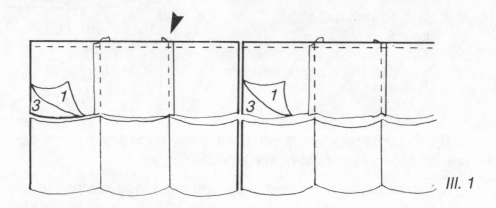

Ill. 1

3. After the first horizontal row of the first block is completed, butt and stitch the first horizontal row of the second block.

4. Continue sewing until the first horizontal row is completed on all blocks.

5. Sew the second horizontal row on all blocks.

6. Snip the threads holding the blocks together.

7. Stack the blocks into one pile.

Chapter 10

Setting the Quilt Top Together with Lattice and Cornerstones

Making the 3½" Cornerstones

1. Follow the Cutting Charts for Lattice and Cornerstones on the following pages for the exact number needed for each individual quilt.

2. Cut the 3½" x 45" strips from selvage to selvage.

3. Press the strips.

4. If you have more than one strip, stack several layers of strips on top of each other.

5. Cut the needed number of 3½" squares.

Ill. 1

Making the Lattice Strips

1. Measure the sides of several completed blocks to find an average measurement. Approximate sizes are:

Monkey Wrench — 12½"

Ohio Star — 12¼"

Bear's Paw — 13¾"

Because each individual's work comes out to their own size, it is important that you measure your own blocks to find an average size.

2. Following the individual charts, cut the required number of 3½" x 45" strips from selvage to selvage.

Economical Suggestion: You can get three lattice strips from a 3½" x 45" piece for all the patterns. However, there is always waste along one side. This excess fabric can be saved.

3. Find the measurement of the lattice strip and multiply it by 3 to find the number of inches they total up to.
Example: 12½" x 3 = 37½"

4. To save fabric, mark over 3 x the measurement of one side on the lattice fabric.

5. Remove this excess side piece to be used later in pillow backs, tote bags, and other sewing projects. Ill. 1

6. Now cut the needed lattice strips from selvage to selvage 3½" x the measured side of the block.

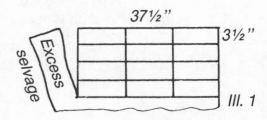

This illustration is just an example and may not be identical to yours.

Cutting Charts for Lattice and Cornerstones

Crib Quilt	Six Blocks
Cut	**To Make:**
Cornerstones: one — 3½" x 45" strips	twelve — 3½" squares
Lattice: six — 3½" x 45" strips	seventeen — 3½" x Finished Size of Block

Lap Robe	Six Blocks
Cut	**To Make:**
Cornerstones: one — 3½" x 45" strips	twelve — 3½" squares
Lattice: six — 3½" x 45" strips	seventeen — 3½" x Finished Size of Block

Twin Quilt	Fifteen Blocks
Cut	**To Make:**
Cornerstones: two — 3½" x 45" strips	twenty-four —3½" squares
Lattice: thirteen — 3½" x 45" strips	thirty-eight — 3½" x Finished Size of Block

Cutting Charts for Lattice and Cornerstones

Double Quilt	Twenty Blocks
Cut	**To Make:**
Cornerstones: three — 3½" x 45" strips	thirty — 3½" squares
Lattice: seventeen — 3½" x 45" strips . . .	forty-nine — 3½" x Finished Size of Block

Queen Quilt	Twenty Blocks
Cut	**To Make:**
Cornerstones: three — 3½" x 45" strips	thirty — 3½" squares
Lattice: seventeen — 3½" x 45" strips . . .	forty-nine — 3½" x Finished Size of Block

King Quilt	Twenty-five Blocks
Cut	**To Make:**
Cornerstones: three — 3½" x 45" strips	thirty-six — 3½" squares
Lattice: twenty — 3½" x 45" strips	sixty — 3½" x Finished Size of Block

Sewing the First and Second Vertical Rows

1. Lay out the patchwork blocks, lattice, and cornerstones according to the size you chose. Follow the illustrations in Chapter 4.

2. Flip the second vertical row right sides together onto the first vertical row. Ill. 1

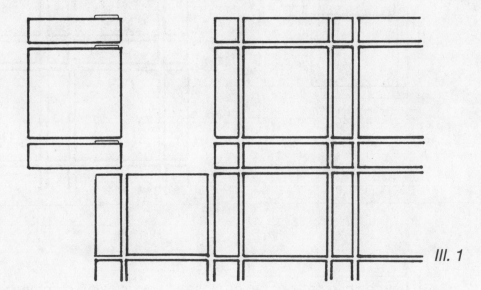

Ill. 1

104

3. Start at the bottom of the first vertical row and stack up the pairs of pieces from the bottom to the top. The first pair will be at the top of your stack. Ill. 1

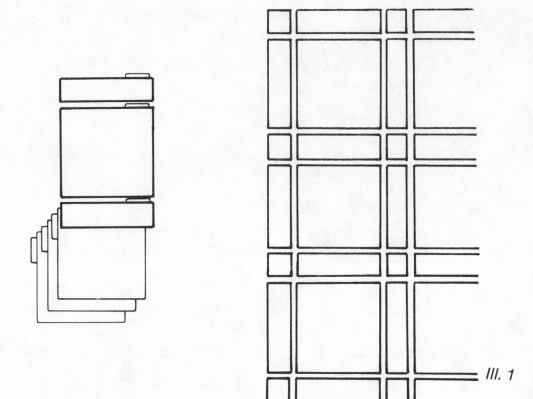

Ill. 1

4. Lay the pile on your lap or close to your sewing machine.

5. Pick up the first lattice/cornerstone pair. Match your edges evenly. The staggering of pieces is purely for illustration purposes. Sew them together.

6. Pick up the lattice/patchwork and flashfeed, anchoring them together with a ½" of back stitching.

7. Match and fingerpin the opposite corner. Stretch them to meet.

8. Stitch.

9. Going down the pile, flashfeed the lattice/cornerstone. Ill. 1

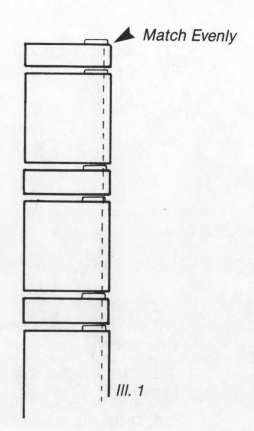

Match Evenly

Ill. 1

10. Continue stitching to the bottom of the row.

11. Accordion fold the pieces starting at the bottom of the row where you just finished sewing to the top of the row.

Sewing the Third Vertical Row

1. Stack up the pieces from the bottom of the row to the top. Place the pile on your lap. Ill. 1

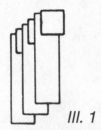

Ill. 1

2. Flip the first cornerstone right sides together onto the lattice strip. Stitch.

3. Flip the lattice strip right sides together to the patchwork block.

4. Anchor them with ½" of stitching. Fingerpin the opposite corners and stretch them to meet.

5. Stitch. Ill. 2

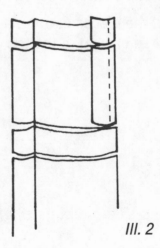

Ill. 2

6. Continue in this manner to the bottom of the row.

7. Finish stitching all vertical rows. Ill. 1 *Do not cut the threads joining the pieces.*

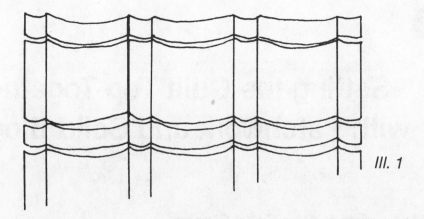

Ill. 1

Lay out the quilt with just its vertical rows stitched. Check to make sure every block, lattice strip, and cornerstone is in its proper position. *It's much easier to rip out now!!*

Sewing the Horizontal Rows

1. Flip the top row right sides together to the second row.

2. Stretch and stitch the patchwork and lattice to meet.

3. At the cornerstones, where the pieces are joined by threads, match the seam carefully. Push the seams in opposite directions toward the dark. Ill. 2

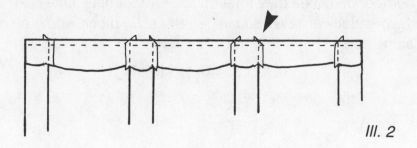

Ill. 2

4. Continue stitching all horizontal rows.

Chapter 11

Setting the Quilt Top Together with Patchwork and Solid Blocks

Measuring for the Solid Blocks

1. Measure several patchwork blocks to find an average finished size. Approximate sizes are:

Monkey Wrench — 12½" square

Ohio Star — 12¼" square

Bear's Paw — 13¾" square

Because each individual's work comes out to their own size, it is important that you measure your own blocks to find an average size.

Economical Suggestion: You can get three solid blocks from a 45" strip for all the patterns. However, there is always waste along one side. This excess fabric can be saved in long pieces for future projects.

2. Multiply the side of the finished patchwork block by 3 to find the number of inches they total up to. For Example: One patchwork block is 12½" square, so the solid block would be cut the same size.

$$12½ \times 3 = 37½" \text{ total}$$

Example

12½" x 3 = 37½" total

3. Mark over 37½" on the solid block fabric. (Ill. 1)

4. Remove the excess side piece to be used later in pillow backs, tote bags, and other sewing projects. Ill. 1

5. Now cut the needed solid blocks from selvage to selvage in strips the width and 3 times the length of the patchwork block. Check your specific bed size for the number of solid blocks you need.

Ill. 1
Example

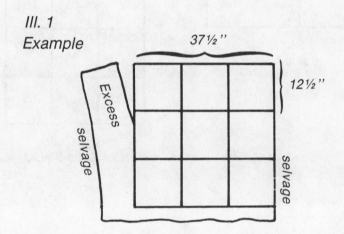

This illustration is just an example and may not be identical to yours. Multiply your patchwork block by 3 to find your measurement.

110

Sewing the Patchwork and Solid Blocks into One Top

1. Lay out your selected size following the corresponding illustration. The numbers indicate the order the blocks are sewn together. The shaded blocks represent the patchwork blocks.

1	2	7
3	4	8
5	6	9

Crib Quilt
4 Solid Blocks

1	2	9
3	4	10
5	6	11
7	8	12

Lap Robe
6 Solid Blocks

1	2	13
3	4	14
5	6	15
7	8	16
9	10	17
11	12	18

Twin Quilt
Nine Solid Blocks

1	2	13	19	25
3	4	14	20	26
5	6	15	21	27
7	8	16	22	28
9	10	17	23	29
11	12	18	24	30

Double and Queen Quilt
Fifteen Solid Blocks

1	2	13	19	25	31
3	4	14	20	26	32
5	6	15	21	27	33
7	8	16	22	28	34
9	10	17	23	29	35
11	12	18	24	30	36

King Quilt
Eighteen Solid Blocks

2. Flip the second vertical row right sides together onto the first vertical row.

3. Pick up the pairs of blocks in the first vertical row from the bottom to the top. The pair at the top will be on the top of the stack. Ill. 1

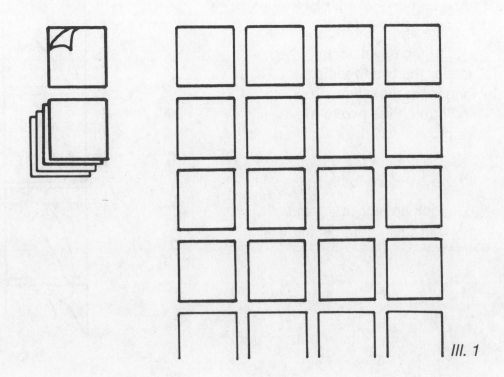

Ill. 1

4. Stack up each one of the vertical rows from the bottom to the top, having the top block on the top of the stack each time. Ill. 2

Example Illustration: Your quilt may not have as many rows.

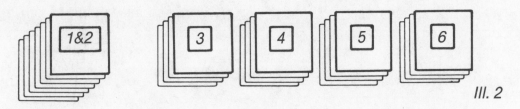

Ill. 2

Write the row number on a small piece of paper and pin it through all thicknesses of fabric.

Sewing the First Two Vertical Rows

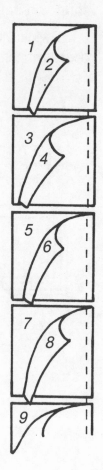

1. Start in the upper left hand corner. Pick up blocks #1 and #2.

2. Stitch down about ½" to anchor the two together. Finger pin the other corner and stretch the two to meet. Stitch.

3. Do not cut the threads or lift the pressure foot.

4. Pick up blocks #3 and #4. Butt them right behind the first two.

5. Anchor the two with ½" of stitching. Fingerpin the corners as before. Stretch the two to meet. Stitch.

6. Continue butting on #5 and #6 in the same manner.

7. Continue butting and stitching until all the blocks in the two rows are completed.

Do not cut the blocks apart.

113

Sewing the Third Vertical Row

1. Place the block at the top of the third vertical row right sides together to #2.

2. Stretch and stitch the two to meet. Ill. 1

3. Butt, stretch, and stitch the second block in the third vertical row onto #4.

4. Butt, stretch, and stitch the third block in the third vertical row onto #6.

5. Continue sewing all blocks in all vertical rows in the same manner. Ill. 2

Do not clip the threads holding the blocks together.

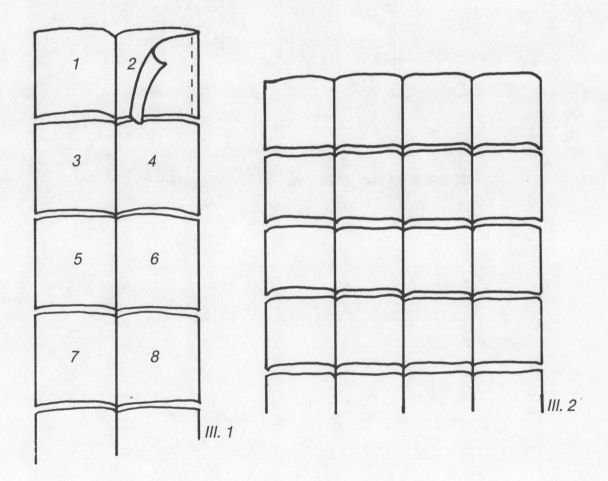

Ill. 1

Ill. 2

Example Illustration — Yours may look different according to the size of quilt.

Sewing the Horizontal Rows

1. Flip the top row down onto the second row with right sides together.

2. Stretch and stitch the pieces to meet. Where the two pieces are joined by a thread, match the seam carefully. Push one seam allowance up on one side, and one down on the other side. Ill. 1

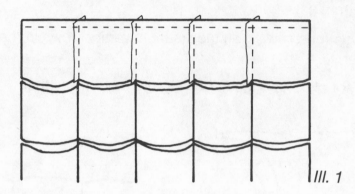

Ill. 1

3. Stitch all horizontal rows in the same manner.

Chapter 12

Sewing the Borders

Follow the Individual Cutting Charts for Borders to make your strips from selvage to selvage: Pages 120 to 125.

Making the  **:**

1. Seam the 4½" x 45" strips of each color into long strips by flashfeeding. *The strips for the queen size quilt only are 5½" x 45".)*

Lay the first strip right side up. Lay the second strip right sides to it. Ill. 1

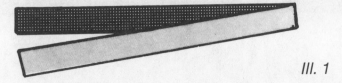

Ill. 1

2. Stitch the 4½" ends together. Ill. 2 *(Queen — 5½")*

Ill. 2

3. Take the strip on the top and fold it so the right side is up. Ill. 3

Ill. 3

116

4. Place the third strip right sides to it. Stitch. Ill. 1

Continue flashfeeding all the 4½" ends together into long strips for each color.

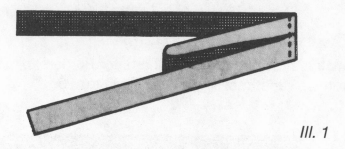

Ill. 1

5. Clip the threads holding the strip together.

6. Seam the long pieces together lengthwise. Ill. 2

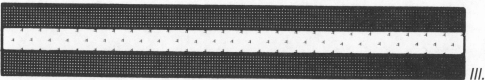

Ill. 2

7. Measure the long sides of the quilt and cut two border pieces the same size.

8. Measure the short sides of the quilt and cut two border pieces the same size.

9. Sew the two long border pieces to the two long sides of the quilt top with right sides together. Unfold.

Making the  **:**

1. Seam the 36" strips together lengthwise. Press the seams flat toward the dark side. Ill. 1 *(Queen — 44")*

Ill. 1

2. Cut into eight — 4½" strips. Stack. Ill. 2 *(Queen — 5½" strips)*

Ill. 2

3. Seam the 18" pieces together lengthwise. Press the seams flat toward the dark side. Ill. 3 *(Queen — 22")*

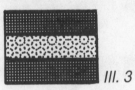

Ill. 3

4. Cut into four — 4½" strips. Stack. Ill. 4 *(Queen — 5½" strips)*

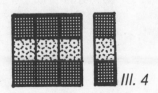

Ill. 4

118

5. Lay the stacks in this pattern next to your sewing machine.
Ill. 1

Ill. 1

6. Assembly line sew all four "nine patch" patterns together.
Ill. 2

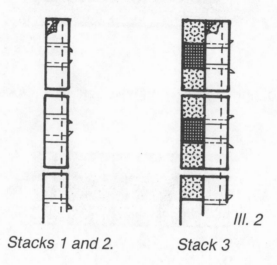

Ill. 2

Stacks 1 and 2.   *Stack 3*

7. Sew a "nine patch" pattern onto each end of the two short border strips. Ill 3.

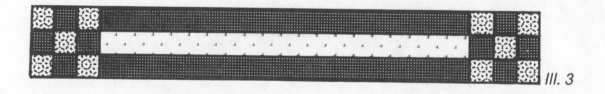

Ill. 3

8. Sew these strips onto each short end of the quilt.

Crib Quilt with Lattice and Cornerstones

Cut. . . . . .To Make:

There are no borders on this quilt.

Crib Quilt with Patchwork and Solid Blocks

Cut. . . . . .To Make:

four — 4½" x 45" dark . . . . .4 ▓▓▓▓▓▓▓▓▓▓▓▓▓▓▓▓

Measure the side of the finished quilt top. Cut the four strips the same size. Seam two border strips to two opposite sides.

one — 5" x 10" light calico
one — 5" x 10" medium calico . . . . .5" ◩◪ . . .4 ◩

Refer to pages 33-34 to make the 4 ◩. Make 5" squares.

Stitch a ◩ on the ends of the remaining two border strips. Stitch the two border strips to the quilt top.

120

Lap Robe with Lattice Strips and Cornerstones

Cut . . . . .To Make:

five — 4½" x 45" light
ten — 4½" x 45" dark . . . .

one — 4½" x 36" dark
two — 4½" x 36" medium 8

two — 4½" x 18" dark
one — 4½" x 18" medium 4

4

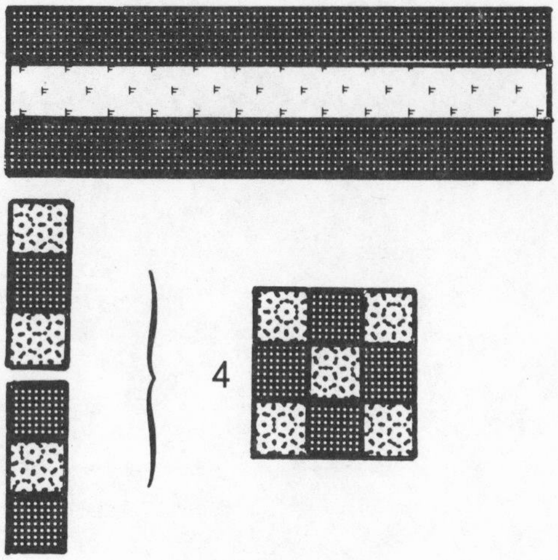

Lap Robe with Patchwork and Solid Blocks

Cut . . . . .To Make:

five — 4½" x 45" light
ten — 4½" x 45" dark . . . .

one — 4½" x 36" dark
two — 4½" x 36" medium 8

two — 4½" x 18" dark
one — 4½" x 18" medium 4

4

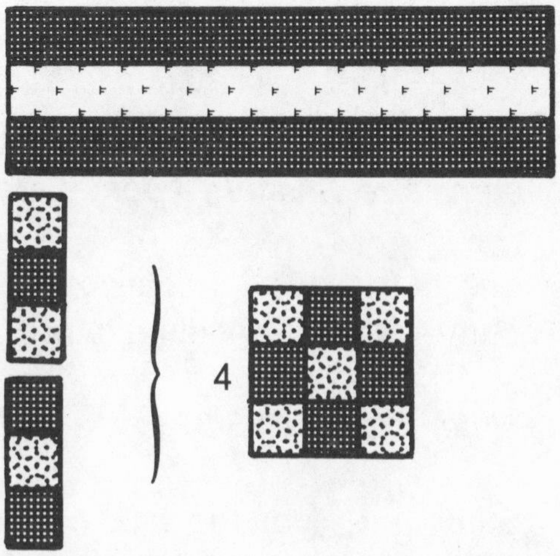

Twin Quilt with Lattice Strips and Cornerstones

Cut . . . .**To Make:**

eight — 4½" x 45" light
sixteen — 4½" x 45" dark . . . .

one — 4½" x 36" dark
two — 4½" x 36" medium 8

two — 4½" x 18" dark
one — 4½" x 18" medium 4

{ 4

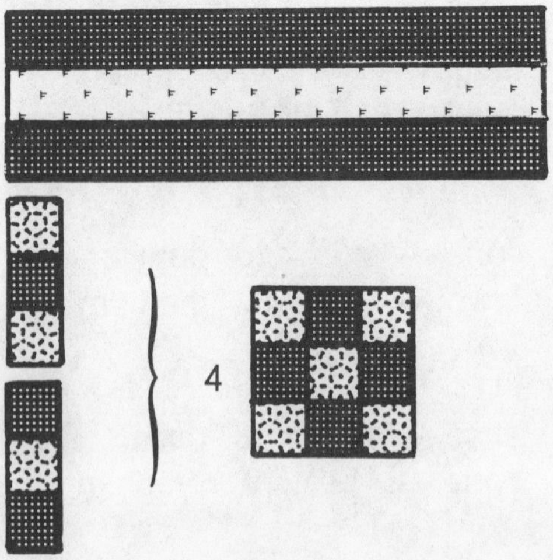

Twin Quilt with Patchwork and Solid Blocks

Cut . . . .**To Make:**

six — 4½" x 45" light
twelve — 4½" x 45" dark . . . .

one — 4½" x 36" dark
two — 4½" x 36" medium 8

two — 4½" x 18" dark
one — 4½" x 18" medium 4

{ 4

122

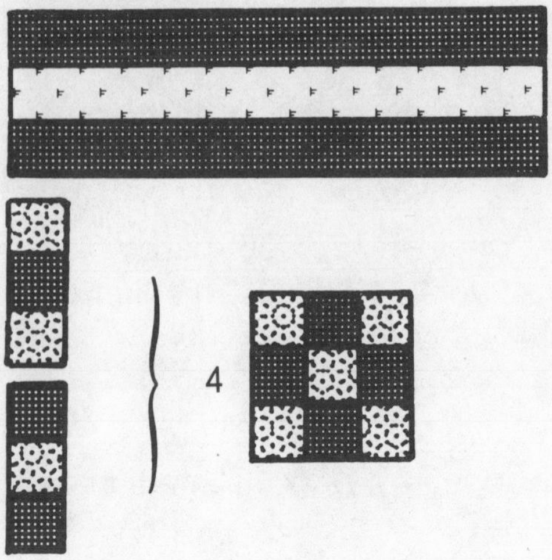

Double Quilt with Lattice Strips and Cornerstones

Cut . . . . To Make:

eight — 4½" x 45" light
sixteen — 4½" x 45" dark . . . .

one — 4½" x 36" dark
two — 4½" x 36" medium 8

two — 4½" x 18" dark
one — 4½" x 18" medium 4

} 4

Double Quilt with Patchwork and Solid Blocks

Cut . . . . To Make:

eight — 4½" x 45" light
sixteen — 4½" x 45" dark . . . .

one — 4½" x 36" dark
two — 4½" x 36" medium 8

two — 4½" x 18" dark
one — 4½" x 18" medium 4

} 4

Cutting Charts for Borders (continued)

Queen Quilt with Lattice Strips and Cornerstones

Cut . . . . **To Make:**

eight — 5½" x 45" light
sixteen — 5½" x 45" dark . . . .

one — 5½" x 44" dark
two — 5½" x 44" medium 8

two — 5½" x 22" dark
one — 5½" x 22" medium 4

} 4

Please note that the block size and layout has been identical in both the double and queen sized quilts. In the border measurements, however, the queen is 6" larger than the double.

Queen Quilt with Patchwork and Solid Blocks

Cut . . . . **To Make:**

eight — 5½" x 45" light
sixteen — 5½" x 45" dark . . . .

one — 5½" x 44" dark
two — 5½" x 44" medium 8

two — 5½" x 22" dark
one — 5½" x 22" medium 4

} 4

124

Cutting Charts for Borders (continued)

King Quilt with Lattice Strips and Cornerstones

Cut . . . . To Make:

nine — 4½" x 45" light
eighteen — 4½" x 45" dark . . . .

one — 4½" x 36" dark
two — 4½" x 36" medium 8

two — 4½" x 18" dark
one — 4½" x 18" medium 4

4

King Quilt with Patchwork and Solid Blocks

Cut . . . . To Make:

nine — 4½" x 45" light
eighteen — 4½" x 45" dark . . . .

one — 4½" x 36" dark
two — 4½" x 36" medium 8

two — 4½" x 18" dark
one — 4½" x 18" medium 4

4

Chapter 13

Finishing Your Quilt

Piecing the Backing Fabric

1. Measure the finished size of your quilt. The backing is to be cut exactly the same size as the finished quilt top.

2. The backing may need to be pieced to get the desired length and width.

3. Divide the width of the quilt top by 42" to discover how many widths are needed.

For example: The quilt measures 72" x 102"

$$\begin{array}{r} \text{app. 2 widths} \\ 42"\overline{\smash{\big)}\,72"} \end{array}$$

Cut two lengths 102" long. There will be extra fabric on the long sides that will need to be trimmed.

4. Cut as many lengths as needed to get the desired width.

5. Seam the pieces together lengthwise.

For best wear on the backing fabric, you may choose to piece this way:

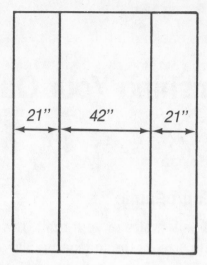

21" 42" 21"

The seams would lay on the sides of the bed and would not get continual stress.

If you are going to embroider your name and date on the back of your quilt, the backing fabric will now fit easily into a hoop. Consider adding your state also as many quilts end up traveling about the country.

Adding Pregathered Lace to the Outside Edge (Optional)

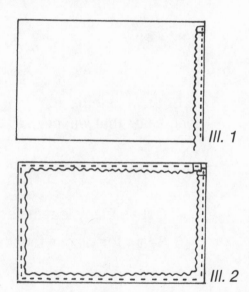

1. Beginning ¼" in at one corner, place the lace right sides together to the quilt top. Fold back the lace ½" at the corner. Ill. 1

Ill. 1

2. Stitch the lace around the outside edge.

3. At the end fold back the lace ½", and cut off. Stitch. Ill. 2

Ill. 2

4. When the quilt is turned right side out, handstitch that corner of the lace.

Sewing the Quilt Top to the Backing

1. Place the backing and the quilt top right sides together.

2. Pin.

3. Trim any excess backing fabric so all sides are even.

4. Stitch around the outside edge with a ¼" seam allowance and 15 stitches per inch.

5. Leave an opening in the middle of one long side approximately 24" long. Ill. 1

6. Lay the quilt top/backing on the floor or on a large table.

Ill. 1

Piecing the Batting

1. Roll out the batting on top of the quilt top/backing.

2. Cut the batting to match up with the seam line. *If the outline of the quilt is too hard to see and trim from, flip all three layers over and trim with the quilt on the top and the batting on the bottom.*

3. The batting may need to be pieced to get the desired size. Cut and butt the two edges closely together. *Do not overlap the batting.*

4. Whipstitch the edges together with a double strand of thread. Do not pull the threads tightly. This will create a hard ridge visible on the outside of the quilt. Ill. 2

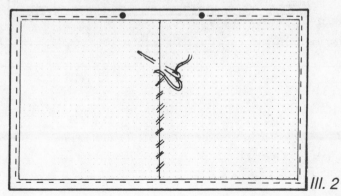

Ill. 2

Turning the Quilt Top

This part of making your quilt is particularly exciting. One person can turn the quilt alone, but its so much fun to turn it into a 10 minute family or neighborhood event with three or four others.

Read the whole chapter before beginning!

1. The three layers are now stacked like this: Ill. 1

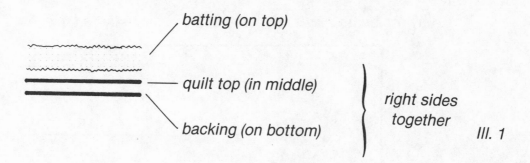

batting (on top)

quilt top (in middle)

backing (on bottom)

right sides together

Ill. 1

2. If you are working with a group, station the people at the corners of the quilt. If working alone, start in one corner opposite the opening. Ill. 2

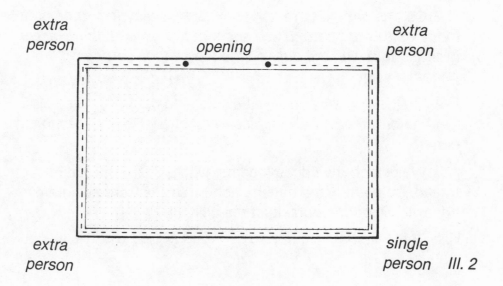

extra person

opening

extra person

extra person

single person   Ill. 2

129

3. Begin at the corners opposite the opening. The corners should look like this: Ill. 1

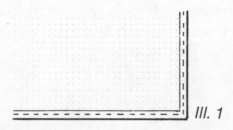

Ill. 1

4. Roll the corners tightly to keep the batting in place. Begin rolling toward the opening. Ill. 2

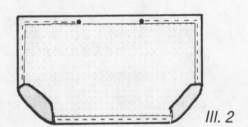

Ill. 2

If several people are helping, all should roll toward the opening. If only you are doing the rolling, use your knee to hold down one corner while stretching over to the other corners.

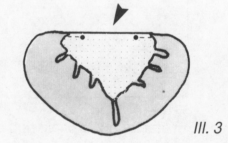

5. Roll all corners and sides towards the opening. Ill. 3

Ill. 3

6. Open up the opening over this huge wad of fabric and batting and pop the quilt right side out through the hole.

7. Unroll it right side out very carefully with the layers together.

8. Lay the quilt out flat on the floor or on a very large table. Smooth out all wrinkles and bumps.

9. Relocate any batting by reaching inside the quilt through the opening with a yardstick. Check to see that the batting goes out to the corners and sides. You can also hold the edges and shake the batting into place if necessary.

10. Whipstitch the opening shut.

"Stitch in the Ditch" the Borders (Optional)

For more dimensional borders, you may choose to "stitch in the ditch" around them rather than tie them.

1. Change your stitch length to 10 stitches per inch.

2. Match your bobbin color of thread to your backing color.

3. Pin along the outside edge and the inside rows.

4. Place the needle in the depth of the seam and stitch. Ill. 1

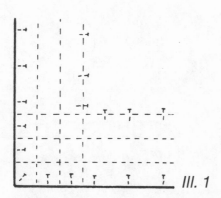

Work from the outside border in toward the center of the quilt.

Ill. 1

5. You can avoid puckering on the back by:

a. running your hand underneath to feel for puckers

b. grasping the quilt with your left hand above the sewing machine foot

c. grasping the quilt with your right hand 10" below the sewing machine foot

d. stretching between the two as you stitch

6. To further avoid puckering on the back, you may choose to use an even feed foot or walking foot, available for most sewing machines.

Tying Down the Quilt Top

A good quality of bonded batting does not fall apart with use or when the quilt is washed. Tying every 12"-15" will serve its purpose of holding the three layers together. However, the more often you tie, the more dimensional looking the quilt becomes.

The following illustrations suggest where to tie each pattern. You can choose how much time you wish to spend on tying.

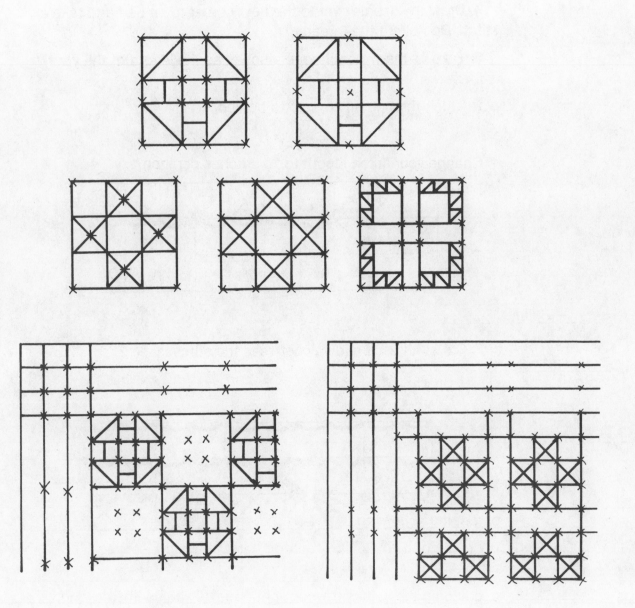

132

Tying a Surgeon's Square Knot

1. Use a curved needle from a packaged assortment of needles. Tie with all six strands of embroidery floss, pearl cotton, wool yarn, or crochet thread.

2. Thread the needle with a long strand for multiple tying.

3. Working from the center out, take a stitch through all thicknesses in one corner. Do not cut the threads.

4. Draw the needle over to the next corner to be tied and take a stitch. Do not cut the threads.

5. Take as many continuous stitches as the length of the yarn will allow.

6. Stitch through all corners to be tied. Ill. 1

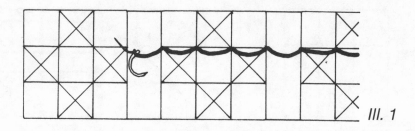

Ill. 1

7. Cut all threads midway between the stitches. Ill. 2

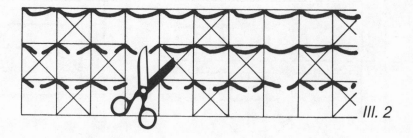

Ill. 2

8. Tie the yarn into surgeon's square knots.

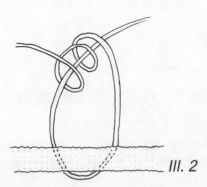 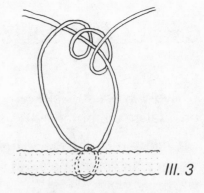

Right over left. Wrap twice.
Draw tight. Ill. 2

Left over right. Wrap twice,
Draw tight. Ill. 3

9. Clip the strands of yarn even to whatever length you wish.

Tying Variations

Tying with 1/16" Narrow Ribbon

For a decorative look on crib quilts, use a narrow 1/16" ribbon. Tie the long strands into tiny bows.

Tying with Buttons and Floss

1. On the right side of the quilt, place a pin through all thicknesses at every corner you wish to tie.

2. Flip the quilt over to the wrong side.

3. At every pin, stitch with a straight needle threaded with floss to the right side. Catch the button, and stitch to the wrong side again.

4. Clip the threads.

5. Tie a surgeon's square knot on the wrong side.

Chapter 14

Care of Your Quilts

Avoid direct sunlight on your quilts to maintain the beautiful original colors of the 100% cotton calicos.

Children's quilts made from preshrunk fabrics can be machine washed and machine dried after construction on a delicate cycle with cold water.

If you wish your colors to remain bright, they can be hand washed in a bathtub using a gentle detergent especially prepared for washing quilts. Do not agitate them, but let them soak in an accordian fold in the tub. After washing and rinsing, remove most of the water by sponging them with towels or mattress pads. Let the quilt dry on a surface where the air can circulate around it. You can create your own drying rack by running poles between the backs of chairs. If the quilt fits in the dryer, I like to give them a final "fluff."

If you wish to hang your quilt as a wall decoration, the safest way to avoid distortion is to sew a casing on the back. See page 138 for more information. Sew this casing onto the backing before adding the quilt top and batting. Draw a rod through the casing and hang it over two nails pounded in at angles.

Chapter 15

Decorating the Country Way

Ohio Star Wallhanging or Small Tablecloth
Approximate finished Size: 34¼" x 34¼"

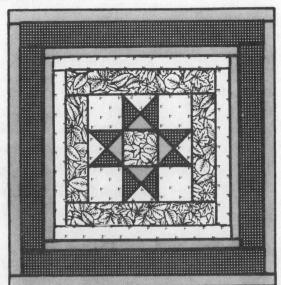

Materials Needed:

⅜ yd. — Light Calico
⅓ yd. — Medium Calico
⅝ yd. — First Dark
½ yd. — Second Dark

1¼ yds. — Backing
2 skeins — Embroidery floss
1¼ yds. — Batting (Wallhanging only)
4 yds. — pregathered, wide lace (optional)
1" dowel rod and two nails (wallhanging only)

Cut . . . . .To Make:

Ohio Star Block

one — 6½" square light calico
one — 6½" square medium calico
two — 6½" square first dark calico 4

four — 5½" squares light calico
one — 5½" square second dark calico . . . .

Borders:

First Border — Second Dark Calico

two — 3½" x approximately 16"
two — 3½" x approximately 22"

Fourth Border — First Dark Calico

two — 4" x approximately 29"
two — 4" x approximately 35"

Second Border — Light Calico

two — 2½" x approximately 22"
two — 2½" x approximately 26"

Fifth Border — Medium Calico

two — 2" x approximately 35"
two — 2" x approximately 38"

Third Border — Medium Calico

two — 2" x approximately 26"
two — 2" x approximately 29"

Casing — Wallhanging Only

one — 5" x 33" strip of backing

Making the Star:

1. Sew the star following the instructions on page 55.

Sewing the Borders:

1. First Border: Place the short strips of the second dark calico right sides together to the Star on two opposite sides. Stitch. Trim the border strips to match the sides. Fold out. Ill. 1

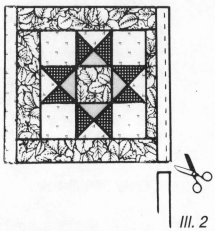

III. 1

2. Place the two longer strips of the first border right sides together to the star on the two remaining sides. Stitch. Trim the border strips to match. Fold out.

3. Second Border: Place the two short strips of the light calico right sides together to the star on two opposite sides. Stitch. Trim the border strips to match the sides. Fold out. Ill. 2

III. 2

4. Place the two longer strips of the light calico right sides together to the star on the two remaining sides. Stitch. Trim the border strips to match the sides. Fold out.

5. Continue adding all borders as in the first and second borders.

6. (Optional) Stitch the lace around the outside edges.

Sewing the Backing for the Tablecloth:

1. Cut the backing exactly the same size as the Star with borders.

2. Place the backing and the Star with borders right sides together.

3. Stitch around the outside edge, leaving a 8" opening on one side.

4. Turn right side out.

5. Whipstitch the opening shut.

6. Tie the Star and borders with embroidery floss. (see page 132)

Sewing the Backing for the Wallhanging:

1. Cut the backing exactly the same size as the Star with borders.

2. Casing: approximately 4" x 33" Stitch the short ends. Ill. 1

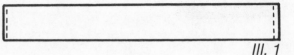

Ill. 1

3. Pin the casing right sides together to the backing 3" from the top edge. Stitch the long side. Ill. 2

Press up and even with the top edge.

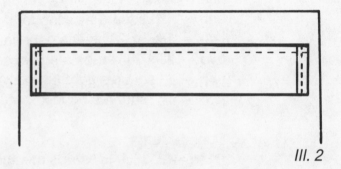

Ill. 2

4. Place the backing and the Star with borders right sides together.

5. Stitch around the outside edge.

6. Leave an opening in the middle of one side approximately 10" long.

7. Lay the Star top/backing on the floor or on a table.

8. Place batting on top of the Star top/backing.

9. Cut the batting to match up with the seam line. If the outline of the quilt is too hard to see and trim from, flip all three layers over and trim with the quilt on the top and the batting on the bottom.

10. Turn the wallhanging (see pages 129-131).

11. Whip stitch the opening shut.

12. Tie down the Star top (see page 132).

13. Cut the dowel rod to extend beyond the casing 1" on both sides.

14. Mark the placement for the two nails and hammer them in at an angle.

15. Hang the ends of the dowel rod over the nails.

138

Toss Pillow with Mock Double Ruffle for Monkey Wrench and Ohio Star

Materials Needed:

Pillow
one — finished Monkey Wrench or Ohio Star Block
one — 17" square backing fabric
two — 1¾" x 28" strips dark calico
two — 2" x 26" strips medium calico
two — 6" squares light or 2nd medium   (four corners)
two — 17" squares bonded batting

Double Ruffle
three — 3½" x 45" strips medium calico (outer ruffle)
three — 2½" x 45" strips dark calico (inner ruffle)

Polyester Stuffing

Making the Pillow Front

1. Center the finished quilt block right side up on the bonded batting. Pin in place. Ill. 1

Ill. 1

2. "Stitch in the Ditch" around the block. Use 10 stitches per inch. Starting at the dot follow the arrows and pivot at the corners. You can stitch continuously around the block without removing it from the sewing machine. Ill. 2

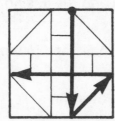 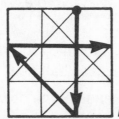

Ill. 2

3. Lay the first dark strip along one side of the patchwork with right sides together. Stitch. Open right side up. Trim the strip even with the batting. Ill. 1

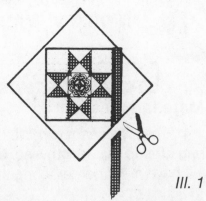

Ill. 1

4. Working in a clockwise direction, rotate to the next side of the patchwork. Lay the next strip right sides together. Stitch. Open right side up. Trim the strip even with the batting. Ill. 2

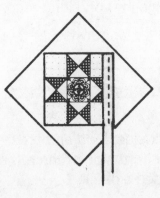

Ill. 2

5. Stitch on all dark strips in the same manner.

6. Stitch on all medium strips. Ill. 3

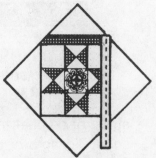

Ill. 3

7. Cut the two — 6" light squares in half. Ill. 4

8. Sew the four pieces to the corners. Ill. 5

Ill. 4

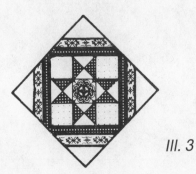

Ill. 5

9. Trim the excess batting.

140

Making the Mock Double Ruffle

1. Seam the three — 45" medium strips into one long strip.

2. Seam the three — 45" dark strips into one long strip.

3. Seam the two long strips together lengthwise. Ill. 1

Ill. 1

4. Press the seam toward the dark side. Fold and press the long strip in half lengthwise. On the front side of the ruffle, you will have a ½" border along the folded side. Ill. 2

◄ Fold

Ill. 2

5. Seam the short ends so the strip is one continuous circle.

6. On the back side of the ruffle, lay a string or crochet thread ¼" from the raw edge. Zigzag over the string being careful not to catch the string. Ill. 3

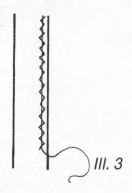

Ill. 3

7. Fold the strip into 8 equal parts. Mark each part with a pin.

8. Pin the ruffle right sides together to the pillow front, matching the middle and corner of each side.

9. Working on ⅛ of the ruffle at a time draw up the cord, space the gathers evenly, and stitch. Ill. 4

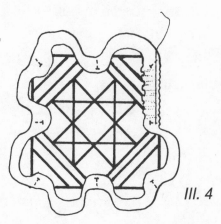

Ill. 4

Finishing the Pillow

1. Place the backing of the pillow right sides together to the front. Trim the backing to fit.

2. Stitch around the outside edge, leaving a 6" opening on one side.

3. Turn right side out.

4. Slip the extra piece of batting into the inside of the pillow. Push the corners of the batting into the corners of the pillow.

5. Stuff in between the two layers of batting. (Pieces of batting trimmed from the quilt and shredded can be used for stuffing.)

6. Whipstitch the opening shut.

Toss Pillow with Mock Double Ruffle for the Bear's Paw

Materials Needed

Pillow
one — finished Bear's Paw Block
one — 17" square backing fabric
two — 17" squares bonded batting
four — 2" x length of finished block dark calico strips
four — 2" squares light calico

Double Ruffle
three — 2½" x 45" medium calico (inner ruffle)
three — 3½" x 45" light calico (outer ruffle)

Polyester Stuffing

Making the Pillow Front

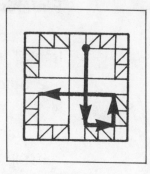

III. 1

1. Center the finished quilt block right side up on the bonded batting. Pin in place.

2. "Stitch in the Ditch" around the block. Use 10 stitches per inch. Starting at the dot, follow the arrows and pivot at the corners. You can stitch continuously around the block without removing it from the sewing machine. III. 1

3. Lay the first two dark strips along opposite sides of the patchwork with right sides together. Stitch. Open both right sides out. III. 2

III. 2

4. Stitch the four 2" light squares onto the short ends of the remaining dark strips. III. 3

III. 3

5. Lay these two dark strips along opposite sides of the patchwork with right sides together. Carefully match the corners. Stitch. Open both right sides out. III. 4

6.. Refer to Making the Mock Double Ruffle on page 141 and Finishing the Pillow on page 142 to complete your project.

Match carefully

III. 4

Hostess Apron with Patchwork Bibb:
Monkey Wrench, Ohio Star, and Bear's Paw

Buy: . . . .**Amount:**

Medium or dark calico fabric . . . . . 1⅝ yds.

(Includes medium or dark fabric
for use in patchwork, but you must
first cut out your pieces according
to the diagram on the next page.)

Pre-gathered lace, ¾" to 1" wide. 2½ yds.

Lightweight batting . . . . 10" sq.

The patchwork block is in reduced scale.
Select one pattern from the following cutting charts.

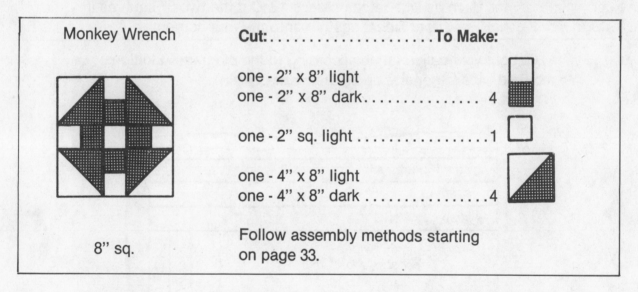

Monkey Wrench

8" sq.

Cut: . . . .**To Make:**

one - 2" x 8" light
one - 2" x 8" dark 4

one - 2" sq. light 1

one - 4" x 8" light
one - 4" x 8" dark 4

Follow assembly methods starting
on page 33.

Ohio Star

9" sq.
(good size to
use for larger
apron)

Cut: . . . .**To Make:**

one - 4½" sq. light
one - 4½" sq. medium
two - 4½" sq. dark 4

one - 3½" sq. dark 1

four - 3½" sq. light 4

Follow assembly methods starting
on page 55.

Bear's Paw (makes one paw only)
Color recommendation: Make the rosebud variation described on page 74.

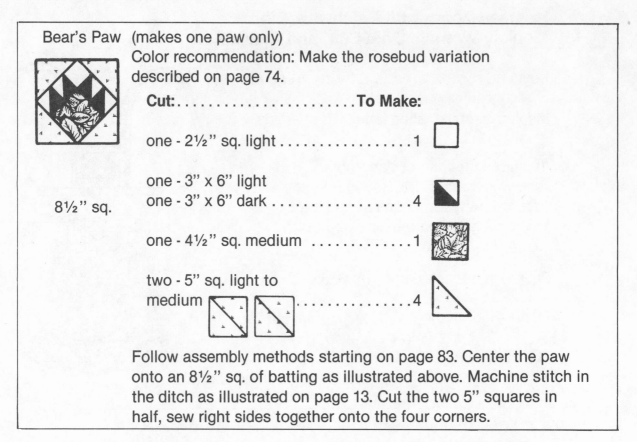

8½" sq.

Cut: . . . . **To Make:**

one - 2½" sq. light 1

one - 3" x 6" light
one - 3" x 6" dark 4

one - 4½" sq. medium 1

two - 5" sq. light to
medium 4

Follow assembly methods starting on page 83. Center the paw onto an 8½" sq. of batting as illustrated above. Machine stitch in the ditch as illustrated on page 13. Cut the two 5" squares in half, sew right sides together onto the four corners.

Cut out your calico fabric according to the diagram. Additions required for a larger size apron are marked with *.

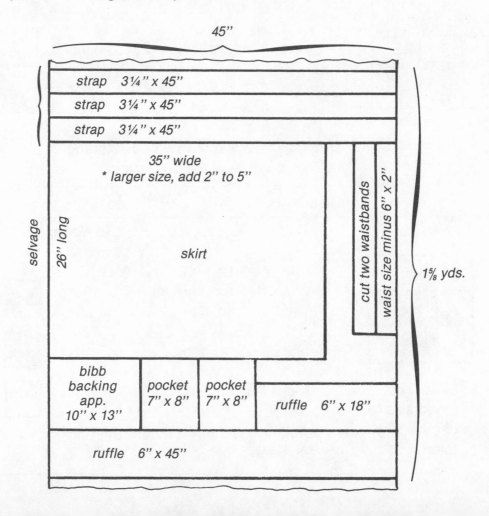

45"

strap   3¼" x 45"
strap   3¼" x 45"
strap   3¼" x 45"

35" wide
* larger size, add 2" to 5"

selvage

26" long

skirt

cut two waistbands

waist size minus 6" x 2"

1⅝ yds.

bibb
backing
app.
10" x 13"

pocket
7" x 8"

pocket
7" x 8"

ruffle   6" x 18"

ruffle   6" x 45"

145

Making the Bibb:

1. Select a patchwork pattern and make one block according to the preceeding scale reduction charts.

2. Cut the batting slightly larger than the size of the completed block. Lay the block on top of the batting. Pin together and machine stitch in the ditch. Refer to the stitching guides on page 13. Trim away the excess batting.

3. Bibb backing: Measure one side of the patchwork and add 3" to the length. The size of your bibb backing will measure the length of one side times the length plus 3". For example, if your patchwork measures 9" square, your backing would measure 9" x 12".

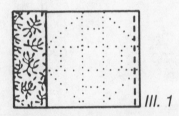

Ill. 1

4. Line up your patchwork along one short side of the backing fabric, right sides together. Pin and stitch along the edge opposite the 3" overlay. Ill. 1

5. Turn right sides out. Line up the two edges at the bottom of the bibb. You should have a 1¼" border across the top of the bibb. Topstitch along the bottom edge of the border. Zig-zag the three raw edges to hold the pieces in place. Ill. 2

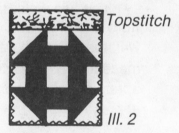

Topstitch

Ill. 2

Making the Straps:

1. Cut one of your three 3¼" x 45" strips in half lengthwise. Stitch each half-strip onto the end of a 45" strip. Ill. 3

Ill. 3

146

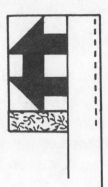

Ill. 1

3. With right sides together, line up one strap along one side of the bibb. Stitch. Ill. 1

4. Repeat with the second strap along the opposite side.

5. Along the remaining raw edges, turn under ¼" and press. Fold in half lengthwise with wrong sides together. Press. Topstitch along the inner edge of both straps. *Ill. 2*

6. Topstitch 1 yard of lace along the outside edges of each strap. Place the lace binding to the back of the strap. Ill. 2

Making the Waistband:

1. Cut two waistband strips: one front and one back. To calculate the waistband length, take the waist measurement and subtract 6". If the apron is a gift, the size can be an approximation.

Ill. 2

Ill. 3

2. Loops: Cut two 2" x 5" strips. With the right side out, press in half lengthwise. Open out and press the two long sides to the center fold line. Ill. 3. Fold in half lengthwise. Press and topstitch the length of both loops.

3. Fold each loop in half. Line up the raw edges along the short ends of the front waistband strip. With right sides together, stitch the loops in place. Ill. 4

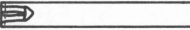

Ill. 4

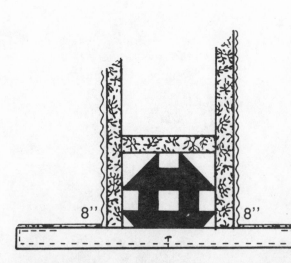

4. Fold the waistband in half to find the center. Pin the center of the waistband to the center bottom edge of the bibb, right sides together. Line up the back waistband strip right sides together behind the bibb backing. Stitch all sides, stopping 8" from the center on the top two sides. Ill. 1

▶ *Notice the strip in back.*

Ill.1

Making the Skirt: (32" wide x 26" long)

1. Pockets: (7" x 8") Stitch lace along one 7" side of each pocket. Turn under the remaining three sides ¼". Pin pockets in place 6" down from top of skirt and 6" in from the sides. Topstitch along the three sides.

2. Ruffle: Sew together the two ruffle strips (6" x 45", 6" x 18") into one long strip. Turn under one length and stitch the hem. Gather the opposite length and stitch it onto the bottom of the skirt.

3. Turn under the two side seams of the ruffle and skirt. Stitch.

Sewing the Skirt to the Bibb:

1. Stitch a long gathering stitch along the top edge of the skirt.

2. Fold the skirt in half to find the center. Mark with a pin.

3. Match the pin to the center of the front waistband only, right sides together.

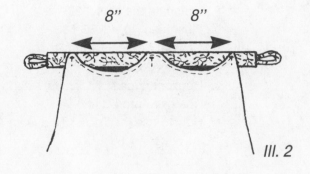

Ill. 2

4. Pin the skirt to the waistband. Ill. 2 (Larger sizes measure 9" to 10" from the center.)

5. Space gathers evenly to fit the waistband. Pin in place and stitch. Turn under the raw edges along front and back waistband. Press. Topstitch.

To tie the apron in the back, cross the two straps, pull through the loops and tie in the middle. Ill. 3.

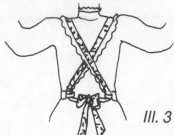

Ill. 3

148

INDEX

BOOK ORDER INFORMATION

If you do not have a fine quilting shop in your area, you may purchase these products from Quilt in a Day™. Please write for a current price list of the books and quilting supplies available. All of Eleanor's books feature full color cover photographs and numerous detailed illustrations. Many include related pattern variations and projects.

#1001 Quilt in a Day (Log Cabin)

Make a beautiful log cabin quilt in 10-16 hours using the speed-sew techniques in this 88 page book. Concise, step-by-step directions with detailed illustrations are presented so even the beginner can find success.

#1002 The Sampler - A Machine Sewn Quilt

Complete, detailed directions and illustrations show how to speed-sew a sampler quilt. The Quilt is assembled using calicos, laces and trims for a nostalgic touch. All 50 patterns are machine quilted on bonded batting for a soft, dimensional look. Instructions for smaller projects are also given.

#1003 Trio of Treasured Quilts

Three different patterns: Monkey Wrench, Ohio Star and Bear's Paw are featured with quick, complete machine sewing methods. Make one block or a whole quilt using the convenient detailed yardage and cutting charts, as well as Eleanor Burns' assembly-line sewing techniques. This book includes projects easy enough for beginners, yet exciting enough for experienced hand quilters.

#1004 Lover's Knot Quilt

The ease of Eleanor Burns' assembly-line sewing techniques continues in the Lover's Knot book. This traditional pattern, resembling the intertwining of two wedding bands, is quick to sew and requires only four colors. Additional features of the book include a sawtooth finished edge and a simple to sew dust ruffle.

#1005 Amish Quilt in a Day

The versatile pattern of the "Roman Stripe" goes together easily with strip sewing and quick cutting of the blocks with a rotary cutter. Full color photographs provide examples of many pattern variations. Also described is a unique "quick-turn" method of showing the backing on the front side and mitering the corners.

#1006 Irish Chain in a Day

Quick strip sewing and rotary cutting is all the "Luck of the Irish" you will need to put this quilt together in only a matter of hours. Perfect for a child's first quilt and beginners of all ages, the Single Irish Chain is a joy to create. Experienced sewers will enjoy the more elaborate pattern variation with the Double Irish Chain.

#1009 May Basket Quilt

Yes, even this delightful traditional pattern has not escaped the assembly-line sewing methods of Eleanor Burns. Color it Amish in dark solids or Victorian in light calicos and lace. Even the basket handle is made easy with a quick marking, sewing and pressing technique. Instructions for pillows, shams, and wallhangings included.

#1010 Schoolhouse Wallhanging

Easy strip piecing and assembly-line sewing come together again in the production of this traditional favorite. Absolutely no templates or complicated measuring. Complete, easy to follow directions include four layout variations: Americana Border, Star, Single Lattice, and Framed Block.

#1011 Diamond Log Cabin Tablecloth or Treeskirt

Complete detailed illustrations will guide you through this exciting pattern quickly and the results are sure to brighten up any room. Construction is based on quick assembly-line sewing and strip piecing methods from the Quilt in a Day Log Cabin book. Although the "diamonds" are made easy with rotary cutting on a 60° angle, this project is most rewarding for experienced sewers.

#1012 Morning Star Quilt

In this beautiful traditional design for experienced sewers, an eight pointed star alternates with a chain block. Eleanor explains how to make it via all the quick piecing and assembly techniques that have brought her such renown among quilters.

#1013 Trip Around the World Quilt

Discover the magic of "tubing" and then "unsewing" strips in this perfect beginner book. It is enchanting tied, or for more challenge, it is a fun machine or hand quilted project. Included are instructions on the overlock sewing machine for even quicker quilts.

#1014 Friendship Quilt

The Friendship Quilt book commemorates Quilt in a Day's Tenth Anniversary with the Album Block featured. In addition to Eleanor's easy-to-understand strip piecing instructions, suggestions are given to help you design and assemble your own special Friendship Quilt.

#1015 Dresden Plate Quilt, a Simplified Method, by Wendy Gilbert
Announcing a NEW book from Quilt in a Day!™ Packed with easy to understand and clearly illustrated steps for machine sewing the plates and blocks together, strip piecing a lattice and 9-patch border. This is a fast and simplified method for making the classic Dresden Plate quilt.

#1016 Pineapple Quilt, a Piece of Cake, by Loretta Smith
Our NEWEST book! This traditionally difficult pattern is redrafted for a contemporary look and made easier with modern tools and techniques. For the experienced quiltmaker, it is complete with choice of quilt sizes, yardage charts and easy to follow illustrations and directions. Color photographs inspire an adventure with this Pineapple.

#1030 Creating With Color, by Patricia Knoechel
Written by a former art teacher, this book explains the basic concepts of combining colors in fabrics and designs so that your next quilting project will be a smashing success. Featuring fan quilts and a fan vest, seven additional patterns are taught, plus many small projects.

Additional Patterns and Projects

#1007 Country Christmas Sewing
Sew ten festive decorations with complete full sized patterns and step-by-step directions.

#1008 Bunnies and Blossoms
This delightful book contains full sized patterns and detailed directions for ten quick sewing projects, featuring sock bunnies and their clothes.

#2011 Dresden Placemats
Combine quaint calicos and rickrack or lace for these easy country table decorations. Clear illustrations show how to speed cut and sew 16 wedges together into placemats, pillows and a tea cozy.

2012 Angel of Antiquity
A Victorian angel with a rose in her hair and a doily for her halo, she's perfect for the top of any Christmas tree.

#2015 Log Cabin Wreath
The log cabin wreath is an easy to construct, assembly-line sewn wallhanging. The pattern uses light and dark fabrics to create a wreath which becomes an impressive looking beginner's project.

#2016 Log Cabin Christmas Tree
Perfect for the holidays, this wallhanging can be made in a twinkling. Utilizing assembly-line sewing methods, you will find this a delightful project to warm the Christmas spirit in your home.

#2017 Easy Radiant Star Wallhanging
Amazingly simple due to rotary cutting and strip piecing, this giant star will measure 40" x 40" in just six hours!

#2020 Flying Geese Quilt
Capture the beauty and symmetry of wild geese in flight. This seemingly intricate pattern is made easy thanks to Eleanor Burns' quick-sew methods.

Video Tapes
Take Eleanor home with you! You can replay her at each step of quilt making as many times as you need in the comfort and convenience of your own home. Her enthusiasm is contagious! Available in VHS: Quilt in a Day Log Cabin, Monkey Wrench, Ohio Star, Bear's Paw, Lover's Knot, Amish Quilt, Irish Chain, May Basket, Schoolhouse Wallhanging, Diamond Log Cabin, Morning Star, Trip Around the World, Friendship Quilt, Country Christmas, Log Cabin Christmas Tree and Wreath, and Block Party Series 1 and 2. Check on new titles and current pricing. Encourage your local public library to carry Quilt in a Day™ video tapes.

Supplies
Quilt in a Day™ carries a line of essential supplies for creating professional looking quilts, including: rotary cutters and replacement blades, cutting mats with grids, 6" x 6" mini rulers, 6" x 12" and 6" x 24" rulers, and the 12 1/2" x 12 1/2" Square Up. Also available are quilter's pins, magnetic pin holders, magnetic seam guides, curved needles, invisible thread and bicycle clips.

Call or write Quilt in a Day™
1955 Diamond Street, San Marcos, California 92069 For Information Call (619)591-0081
Orders Only Call 1-800- U2 KWILT (1-800-825-9458) Ask for the Mail Order Department